Lawyer's Guide

To (Virtual) Initial Consults And E-Signed Retainers

By Richard Jacobs & Tracy Merda

Speakeasy Marketing, Inc.
73-03 Bell Blvd, #10
Oakland Gardens, NY 11364
(888) 225-8594
www.SpeakeasyMarketingInc.com

Ordering Information:
Quantity sales. Special discounts are available on quantity purchases by corporations, associations, and others. For details, contact the publisher at the address above.

Orders by U.S. trade bookstores and wholesalers. Please contact Speakeasy Marketing: Tel: (888) 225-8594 or visit www.SpeakeasyMarketingInc.com.

Printed in the United States of America

Published in 2021

ISBN: 978-1-951149-66-6

DEDICATION

In March 2020, when countries', cities', and states' reaction to COVID threw the legal world (and the rest of the world) into the proverbial blender, it forced an immediate and significant re-invention of how to conduct initial consults.

Hopefully soon, things may return to normal, but in case they don't, and in the meantime, if you're unable to use modern technology such as Zoom, Google Meets, Skype, and other video platforms, your chances of closing new potentials will be drastically curtailed.

Tracy and I dedicate this book to the tens of thousands of attorneys who receive our daily, weekly and monthly communications via Speakeasy Marketing and Jacobs and Whitehall.

May you read this book and prosper, in spite of current conditions!

DISCLAIMER

This publication is intended to be used for educational purposes only. No writer-reader relationship is intended to be created by reading this material. The publisher, authors, and all business associates assume no liability for any errors or omissions or for how this book or its contents are used or interpreted or for any consequences resulting directly or indirectly from the use of this book or the material therein.

If you are an attorney, please know that the material in this book may conflict with local, state or federal bar requirements, ethics requirements for being an attorney, or other requirements or laws. Nothing in this book should be construed to be legal, ethical, or otherwise. Your implementation, reliance on, or use of any of the information contained in this book is at your own risk.

Testimonials

"Speakeasy Marketing Is The Best Thing That Has Happened To My Law Practice!"

"I can say unequivocally that Speakeasy Marketing is the best thing that has happened to my law practice! I have been a practicing attorney in New Haven, Connecticut for over 36 years and I have tried so many different marketing methods and firms that I can no longer keep track. Often times, I have been a sucker for pitches that over-promised and under-delivered. These experiences made me gun-shy and I was reluctant to build a website and market my practice anymore. However, Richard made a convincing presentation over the telephone and thereafter in person prompting me to give him a chance. Well, as I said earlier, it was career changing! My website is the envy of my colleagues and my practice is thriving at a time when my peers are struggling. Speakeasy's employees are proactive and suggest changes and improvements all of the time and it is only my laziness that keeps me from helping them do more. They are prompt in replying to questions and they are helpful with all matters of technology that I struggle with. I cannot say enough about Richard and his team! I Hope my Speakeasy Marketing Review helps other fellow clients in their professional practice."

— Jack O'Donnell, Esq.

****

"His Approach To Internet Marketing Is New & Unique"

During the 15 years I have been marketing my website on the internet, I have tried a number of marketing companies none of which achieved the right fit. From big companies to small from individuals to friends and relatives I have continuously sought the personal attention and results I desire. In each instance they talked a "good game" but never delivered winding up as merely glorified hosts for my website.

Richard Jacobs of Speakeasy Marketing Inc. is the real deal. I spoke to him initially out of curiosity and waited all too long to retain his services. I have now been on board for about one year and recommend his services without hesitation. To be more specific he and his team excel in the following areas:

He is always available to answer your questions and concerns. He is acutely aware of my particular needs and individual situation. Because he represents attorneys exclusively, he brings a wealth of knowledge and experience to the intricacies of attorney internet marking. His approach to internet marketing is new and unique and designed to separate you from the "pack".

With his unique approach, I no longer have to continuously worry about the position of my website on the various search engines and can now finally relax and do what I do best, as I know he is the best. For any attorney who is procrastinating about whether to change internet marketing companies and retain Richard, I can only say, "the longer you wait the more clients you will lose to your competitors".

— Michael Kramer, Counselor

****

"My Site Generates Solid Traffic And Great Conversions."

I have been working with Richard Jacobs and Speakeasy for several years now and I can vouch for the effectiveness of his online marketing and SEO system. Content is king and the major search engines do not reward 'shortcuts' anymore.

Original, unique content is what search engines reward with increased ranking. Richard's system of having you 'speak' your own content in the form of practice-specific interviews is hands-down the best – and easiest – way to generate solid, unique content. Too many legal web marketing companies rely on the same old generic canned content for the various practice areas.

That's why so many lawyers and firms fight for mediocre rankings: they are all posting the same generic content that is focused on key-word stuffing rather than unique, detailed narrative content. It took time, patience and steady contributions to content by participating in regular content interviews with Richard's staff. But my site routinely receives over 3,000 unique visitors every month. And I never need to worry about whether my site will take a hit when Google releases its next big SEO Algorithm shake-up!

— Paul D. Cramm, Esq.

****

"My Phone Has Been Ringing And I Have Been Signing Up New Clients."

When it boils down to it the real test of any SEO company is does your telephone ring with calls from good potential clients. Since I have been using Speakeasy, my phone has been ringing and I have been signing up new clients. Richard and the employees at Speakeasy are awesome!!!

— James Alston, Esq.

****

"21 Calls And 6 Retained Clients In 30 Days From Direct Mail Alone."

The past 5 years have been extremely tough – Yellow Pages doesn't work, TV & radio are too expensive, and SEO companies are a dime a dozen. Richard Jacobs started providing DWI leads to my firm, then took over our website from a terrible vendor, redesigned it, and helped me get back on track with my marketing. I used to worry constantly about affording the monthly bills and couldn't figure out what I was doing wrong – Richard has been patient, extremely knowledgeable, and always there when I needed him. My firm is profitable again, and I'm back on track and succeeding. Thank you so much for your help, Rich.

— Eric Sachs, Esq.

****

"Last Year, I Retained 34 Clients From My Website Alone"

Richard Jacobs with Speakeasy Marketing has been an incredible resource for my law firm. We've worked together for nearly 4 years, and in that time, Richard has re-designed and grown my website's traffic exponentially. During my years of marketing companies and vendors, I have found Richard and his company to stand above the rest as being both reliable and responsive.

Being an attorney, I carefully screen who I let work with me, one of the reasons being that ethics are vital to everything I do in my practice and in maintaining my professional license. I've watched Richard's methods and ideas become tremendously more relevant to what real attorneys need to run a successful practice. He's a valuable resource and I highly recommend his SEO, website design, and marketing services to serious attorneys.

— Kevin Leckerman, Esq.

****

TABLE OF CONTENTS

About Me

Before we dive into the content, I'm going to share a bit of my story with you. I'm not an attorney. I've been accused of being one, but I'm not. I want to make that clear that right off the bat. I've never been to law school and unfortunately, I never will. However, my gift and skill set is marketing. I specialize in marketing legal services for small firms, generally one to three attorneys in all practice areas including estate planning, criminal defense, personal injury, family law, real estate, business litigation, and so on. This is my main market and I know it very well.

Like I mentioned, I didn't' go to law school but I take the approach of looking at legal services from the point of view of your clients. I see legal problems, your services, your experiences, and your accolades from the eyes of potentials because I've been one myself. I've needed legal services from time to time throughout my life. For example, I was in a car accident 20 years ago. I filed for bankruptcy once before. I've even had various brushes with the law with traffic tickets. I've done my estate planning and so on. I've had to hire attorneys in six or seven practice areas over the past 20 years or so. I've been a potential and at times, I'm still a potential.

I want to tell you a quick story. When I first started my company, I built myduiattorney.org. We provided DUI leads to attorneys nationwide. All said and done we put out over 35,000 leads over just a few years. Eventually it was sold to a competitor, but we did really well.

I then decided I wanted to go beyond that. I wanted to offer a full suite of marketing services to my attorneys. Just giving them leads wasn't enough. That's why I expanded my services to become Speakeasy Marketing. For nearly 11 years, we have been going strong.

In addition to running Speakeasy Marketing, I've authored several books based on my experiences.

Secrets of Attorney Marketing is now in its third edition. A fourth is on its way in another year or so. I've also done the *Attorney Authority Reboot* book, about creating a Speak a Book. I've been part of the Ultimate Local Guide To Business Marketing and have been invited to speak at the NACDL and the American Bar Association. Additionally, I conducted a webinar for the Young Lawyers Division, and I've had the opportunity to speak at PILMMA and Local Lawyers Meetup Groups about our Speak a Book and about attorney marketing.

We are currently in talks with several bar associations to host a *Virtual Closing System* seminar for some of their people. What I am trying to say, is that I've been around and speaking on the circuit for a while now. It is important to me. I've been in this industry a long time and I know it very well. I've dealt with it from many perspectives for quite a long time. All of this is to say, I have a unique perspective which will help your firm grow, now in the time of the pandemic, as well into the future.

CHAPTER 1

REALITY OF COVID-19

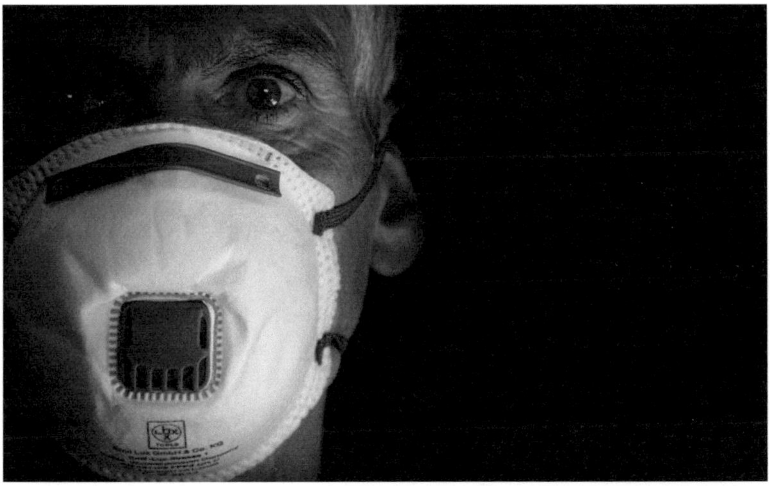

It is no news to anyone that courts were closed and legal services almost ground to a halt this year. Even now, with some areas reopened, practicing law for a lot of people, is a trickle of what it was earlier this year. There are still cases out there to grab, but competition is fierce. A lot of potentials can't or won't come into your office. Even with the quarantine lifted, the coronavirus is still frightening to a lot of people. I see it in the local businesses here in Austin, Texas. No one has guidance on what to do or where you can go. People are going to be afraid and unsure for a long time. Of course, things will go back to normal, but it's going to take some time. So, what does this mean for your practice?

This means, for the foreseeable future, you may need to work on closing potential clients virtually; at least those who aren't comfortable coming in for a face to face appointment. You can't be subpar at this. You need to be good. You need to be effective and efficient. Get those potentials into your virtual office on Zoom, evaluate their case, present your service package, and close them. If you don't, you are going to lose those precious cases to attorneys who've figured out how to do this elegantly using their own virtual closing methods.

There are already big-time winners and big-time losers during the current coronavirus crisis. We are not here to capitalize on it. We respect the fact that this is incredibly serious. However, the message we do want to share is that no matter what, you cannot let your practice fall prey to the fear of this pandemic. In this book, you will learn about unique processes that you can implement in your practice.

I, myself, was caught in the fear in the very beginning of this situation. Then, I spoke to a friend of mine and he asked, "Well, what are you going to do about it?"

He continued, "There is nothing we can do. This is out of anyone's control for the most part. So, are you going to give up or are you going to embrace the situation and figure out how to navigate it and be successful?"

That was like a good slap in the face I needed. From that point on, I figured I decided I was going to take matters into my own hands. I was going to get my business through this and so I began to work on ways to do just and help the attorneys I work with do the same. It's in use and it's working for our attorneys. The great part is that this is not only going to help you through more shutdowns, should they come. It's going to help you in all ways going forward. It's called the *Virtual Closing System*.

My goal with this system, is to give you simple and powerful frameworks for preparing and closing potentials remotely. I am going to share with you a series of simple steps that you can follow to turn calls, emails and live chats into signed retainer agreements when means more revenue. You will learn how to keep your pipeline full of lucrative work, despite the limitations the coronavirus situation has put on your business. I want to take away the frustration you may have been feeling about not being able to physically sit down with potentials and close clients in your office. I will show you how you can replace all of that with a feeling of certainty and confidence by following our *Virtual Closing System* methods.

Can we make this shutdown end? No. I wish we could, and I know you do too. Can we singlehandedly heal the economy? No. What we can do, however, is make sure next time a potential calls you, you have the best possible method to close them and you never have to leave money on the table again. My goal ultimately, is to give you tools that not only keep the wolf from your door and help you survive the shutdown, but also help you thrive in it. I want to help you keep growing your firm even when your competitors are taking on more debt and falling by the wayside. We don't know when this will all end. However, when the world goes back to normal, and it will, you may even want to keep using these methods to keep closing potentials this way. You won't be the only attorney who has come to this conclusion. Believe me.

The *Virtual Close System* is going to save you a lot of time and is an excellent proxy for getting people "in the office", without having to meet in person.

If nothing else, there is one thing I know I can do for you and that is to show you how to convert more leads into signed clients and cashflow, instead of losing them to competitors who are maybe better prepared than you are right now. I'm not going to hold anything back, because I have faith that you are going to use what I show you in this book. When the pandemic began and shutdowns across the country happened, I saw many attorneys fold and close up shop. These were lawyers who before the virus, were doing fantastic. They had been practicing law for 10, 20, 30 plus years and thought they were going to continue toward retirement. Now, sadly, they are gone. They were snuffed out by what is going on in the world and it bothers me.

I personally know what it's like to put everything you have into a business. You spend years of your life watching it grow from nothing into something that provides you and family with a good life. You get to see how your employees and their families get income and make a life for themselves as well. Then one day, poof. It's gone without so much as a warning. I know this pain. It's something I experienced myself many years ago.

I'm going to give you my best in these pages. In return, I ask for you to do the same, while I share these strategies with you.

While you are reading this book, I want you to picture yourself using what I'm going to show you. I want you to see yourself in your mind's eye using this new framework. If you follow these strategies, you will blow the potentials away and present the absolute best of what you and your practice have to offer.

It's time for you to embrace the new world in which we are living in. There is actually a lot of opportunity out there because remember, unfortunately, there are those attorneys who are not going to adapt. They are going to be forced to close down, which will leave more potential clients for you.

These are the attorneys that are saying to themselves, "Oh that won't work for me. In my area of law, and in my state and my area, its different. People are different. This is not going to work."

They are going to find reasons why it can't work for them and they are not going to do it. Instead you have to say to yourself, "How can I use this information to benefit my practice?".

If you have that mindset, you will find ways to use it and you will profit from it. I want you to know, I am going to do my best and I want your best. and your attention.

I truly believe this system is going to help your practice get through this time and come out stronger on the other end. From there it's on and upwards from there. So, let's get started ....

CHAPTER 2

CLOSING POTENTIALS VIRTUALLY

Due to the coronavirus pandemic, right now it may not be possible to meet with people who need your attorney services face to face, in person.

In this chapter I am going to give you quick tips that you can apply right now, regardless of what type of law you practice.

Tips For Attorneys To Close More Potentials

The first thing I want to tell you, is do not try to close potentials over the telephone - pandemic or not. That is what your competitors do. It does not differentiate you and more importantly, it is not highly effective. When you are on the phone with potentials, they can only hear your voice. This is not enough to create a bond and to start gaining their trust. This is why in person consultations are always ideally what every attorney wants when it comes to meeting potential clients.

If you implement nothing else from what I share with you here, this tip alone will increase your closing rate. We have tested this many times with real attorneys and real potentials. That's the first thing. Potential clients need to see you and right now video calls are the best replacement for in person office meetings.

The second thing you need to do to implement a virtual close strategy, is to choose the right video conferencing platform. There are many different programs out there including Skype, FaceTime, Facebook Messenger, Google Hangouts and more.

Personally, I use and recommend Zoom for all video calls and consultations.

I use Zoom for several reasons, including the excellent call quality and reasonable price. It also allows you to seamlessly switch to video call and to screen share back and forth. The latter is vital when it comes time to reviewing your retainer with the potential and getting them to sign right then and there over video.

Additionally, I personally find that Zoom is a secure platform that I trust. It should be noted that with any online system, precautions need to be taken to protect the potential's confidential information, which we will get into in more detail later in the book.

The third thing I want to discuss when it comes to applying the virtual closing method, is the dress code. Even though you may not be meeting with potentials in your office, you still need to dress smart as though you are. Don't make the mistake of dressing sloppy like some attorneys do. I know we are all probably a little guilty of letting it slide these days; wearing our comfy clothes all day long, going unshaven and without haircuts for months. However, potentials expect you to look the part regardless. They respond based on your appearance. It's important to create the sense of authority and some of that is done by dressing and looking the part of an attorney the potential would want to hire.

If I Can Get Them Into My Office, I Know I Can Close Them

I want to talk about a phrase that has been in my head a lot lately, which actually spawned the idea for the *Virtual Close System*. The saying is, "If I can get them into my office, I know I can close them."

I hear those words not only in my head a lot. I also hear them from attorneys all the time. It's true. The magic generally happens when a client or a potential client is in your office. Right now, attorneys need more than just leads right now. They can't always get potentials into the office. Therefore, there must be a better way to ensure you get that opportunity to close. That is the whole purpose of the *Virtual Close System*.

I've heard these words uttered by attorneys for 11 years. The attorneys that told me this, were right. Their marketing problems could be solved if they could get people into the office. However, now you can't get them into the office as often as you would like. So, how do you close them?

You have probably heard a lot about video conferencing in the past few months. Zoom, for example, has exploded with over 300 million people using it. For those of you not familiar with Zoom, I'm going to tell you what it's about and why it's such a powerful tool to have in your arsenal. Additionally, I will talk to you about DocuSign, where you can review agreements and get E-signatures online as well. I use that for our agreements and it's awesome. You can virtually walk through a retainer agreement with a potential, get initials along the way and then get the final signature right then and there. It's a branded technology that works.

Other online tools I am going to suggest you use include screensharing and a virtual whiteboard, which we will get into later. You can also now exchange files, submit signatures and, of course, send and receive payments using PayPal, Venmo, Direct Deposit, checks and more. There are a multitude of ways to do things without physically being with someone nowadays. You can absolutely get clients convinced, a retainer signed and money on its way to you without ever having to meet them physically.

You may have received offers from marketing companies that want to sell you their virtual systems in return for a handsome fee. I want you to save your money which is why I am teaching you how to use these online systems instead.

CHAPTER 3

BE THE AUTHORITY TO YOUR POTENTIAL CLIENT

Technology is great. However, if you don't know how to use it effectively, it doesn't do you any good. There can be a steep learning curve for a lot of people. Just because you have Zoom or DocuSign, doesn't mean you know how to use it effectively. There's a lot more to it to fully take advantage of what these programs can do for you, in combination with other closing elements that must be present as well.

That's part of the magic of this Virtual Closing System which we will get to in just a bit.

For your selling system, there are some overarching elements you have to have in order to be successful. First, you must be the authority to a potential client. You don't want to get through your sales pitch and have the potential client say, "I talked to someone else and he is willing to take my case for half of what you are charging."

You won't hear this if you establish yourself as the authority. Instead you will get respect and you will hear eagerness in the potential's voice. You will know they are sold by the end of that call. In this book, I will tell you how to do this.

The next element you must have is the perfect pitch. You must pitch them in such a way that they can't say no. There are ways to do this over the internet on video. My goal for you, is that you can close most people immediately. You don't want to let them think about or say they will get back to you.

Get The Potentials Right Then And There

You must do everything you can to close potentials while you are with them on video and I'm going to show you how to do that. There are many ways to remove resistance and get them right then and there. For those who you can't sign right on the spot, there are ways to follow up and close maybe a week or two later and further increase your conversion rate. This was ignored for a long time because attorneys thought times were good. The economy was good. Well now, you need every bit of juice out of that orange and I will show you how to do it.

There are five parts to the *Virtual Close System*. I'm going to go through all of them. I want you to get them right. I want you to be equipped with the right technology and know how to use it so you can keep your pipeline stuffed full of the right cases and make money again.

I want your firm running through closings and becoming one of the strong firms that may even thrive during this period. I'm going to explain shortly why meeting potentials online is very efficient. It conserves time and energy and it can be incredibly effective. You don't have to drive anywhere to meet with anyone. They don't have to drive to you. There are so many things that will reduce your conversion rate if people have to get up and go see you. By using the virtual closing system, you will increase your conversion tremendously. Every attorney wants a high conversion, good clients, and real money for the legal work you do. They want less no-shows. They want to stop wasting time on deadbeats. This is why I am going to show you how the Virtual Closing System can work for you.

Five Things You Have To Get Right

There are five things you must get right when it comes to closing potential clients. The first, is that you need to ensure calls coming into your office are answered properly. When I say call, that could be an actual phone call, a live chat, an email, etcetera. You need to first, screen out the price shoppers. Establish your positioning and qualify these people. Then you need to ensure you are preselling them on hiring you before you are even on the line. Your admins can do this. Answering services with scripts can do this. It is absolutely possible when you have the right tools. If you don't set yourself up properly from the beginning with that authority, it's going to be an uphill battle; no matter what technology you have.

The next step that is crucial to your success, is to conduct a case evaluation through screenshare. You will share your screen with the potential through Zoom or whatever platform you choose and show them your online whiteboard. You can also use the camera feature to use a physical whiteboard. As the potential client is answering questions you have asked which are pertinent to their situation, you will be writing the details down on the physical whiteboard or typing it out on your virtual whiteboard. By doing this, you are engaging the potential to participate in their own case. You have captured their attention and now they are building their defense with you. It's going to make it very unlikely that they are going to go with someone else. Why is that? Almost no attorney is doing this. Most are just getting on the phone with a potential and quickly glossing over the details and what to expect in their case, all while the potential sits there gripped with fear. They maybe hear 10% of what is being said. Instead, using the whiteboard method I earlier described to you, the potential is engaged in what you are saying and explaining and relaxed enough to pay attention. You are going to suck them in as they sit there with you going through the visual assessment of their case. When you start to use these methods, you are going to see your conversion skyrocket.

The third thing you must get right when closing clients has to do with how you present your offer to the potential. You need to show them the incredible value they are getting by hiring your firm. You should never just go into a closing with a potential and say, "My fee is X."

In our *Virtual Close System*, you will have an entire script for you to follow and I will teach you how to show the prospective client on your whiteboard, three different prices and where your pricing falls and why. When you do it this way, you are showing the potential client a side by side comparison of you, next to the low-ball attorneys and the incredibly expensive attorneys. It makes the attorneys that offer low fees look like chumps, when they see their services and qualifications next to yours right there in front of their eyes. The same can be said when they see your price and value next to the expensive attorney. They will see that you offer much more, if not all of the same, for a better price. When they have the comparison right there in front of them, you won't have to deal with hearing, "Well, I talked to someone and they will do it for half of what you are quoting."

You won't have to put up with that anymore because I'm going to show you how to remove it from the equation before it even comes up.

The last two parts I want you to master will cover how to close someone right then and there and even get that first payment. I will also tell you how to minimize or remove the stall tactics potentials often use. You know the dreaded phrases and objections I'm talking about that no one wants to hear. They are in every industry.

"Let me talk to my wife," or "I'll need to think about it and get back to you."

I will show you how to stomp that stuff out. We will then talk about even if you can't get them on the spot and you have done your best, why you still don't give up and what to do about it. You aren't going to sign everyone you meet with; it's not likely. However, the key is even if you don't get a yes that day, don't forget to follow up. If you don't you are just throwing your time, energy and good cases in the garbage.

I'm going to teach you about the follow up. However, our *Virtual Close System* even has a program that will do it for you.

You want your follow up to be executed in an ethical, professional way. You don't want to come off as desperate. That gives away your positioning. Your follow up has to be perfected and I will show you how it can be done with the modalities and methods you will learn in this book.

Lastly, I will tell you about the bonus module we have added to the *Virtual Close System.* Anyone who invests in this system is going to get this additional module. It covers offering payment plans and getting your full retainer within 72 hours. The client will be on a payment plan and the finance company would be dealing with the bill chasing; not you. You need to be able to focus on practicing law. Leave the financing to the finance guys.

CHAPTER 4

AN OVERVIEW OF THE 5 STEPS

Step #1: How To Answer Incoming Calls The Right Way

"Law office of so and so."

"He's not here."

"Call back later."

Poor phone etiquette like this is no longer allowed. You have to ensure every time someone calls your office that the phone is answered properly. You need to be able to screen out the price shoppers, establish your positioning and get people pre-sold on you before they even speak to you. Why? Potentials aren't coming into your office as often as they used to. Due to the current circumstance, more often, you are coming into their space now over video.

This changes the dynamic because the potential is not there with you in person and it's the reason why you need to establish authority and gain their respect immediately. You might be 15 minutes into your discussion and if you turn the potential off, they can just say goodbye and click a button. That's it. You've wasted your time. You must establish elevate yourself before you speak to that person so that they treat you right and respect you during the interaction.

One of the ways you can accomplish this, is by using telephone message scripts for answering the phone. You can use one for every possible scenario. What if the call goes to voicemail? What if the admin answers? What if they are on hold? What if an answering service takes the call? What if someone else in your office that doesn't normally pick up the phone answers? What do you say if you answer the phone? How do you position yourself?

All scripts need to be friendly and they have to pre-qualify the potential. This is especially important. For nearly 11 years now, at Speakeasy Marketing, we have done mystery shopping for some of our clients. At the end, we provide them with a written report that analyzes the customer experience according to several different metrics. Most attorneys we provided the reports to were embarrassed and surprised. Some of them didn't know they were missing out on calls and potentially 20%-30% more business. They were frustrated but what they saw. They thought their marketing wasn't working or that they weren't getting calls from good potentials. They didn't know their voicemail message sucked or was non-existent or their receptionist was rude and turned people off. I've heard it all and unfortunately a lot of it is really bad.

I am now going to get into how to do this properly so you can avoid losing potentials who contact your office. Done right, this will open your funnel tremendously.

Step #2: Create An Involvement Device

I've created a case evaluation system which I am going to share with you. This will rivet your potential client. It will let them see you, hear you and will pull everything we are talking about here together. This gives the potential the opportunity to put your name with your face and voice. They will see your mannerisms and gestures, while at the same time hearing your knowledge and expertise regarding your case. With the methods I am going to show you, you will be recreating yourself in person, albeit you will be on video.

To do your job, you have to get critical pieces of information from the potential. However, from the closing point of view, the way you conduct this is critical. You have to get the client to believe in you and to know you are competent. They need to feel that you are going to do a good job for them, that they can afford you and make them want to work with you. You need to get the potential to feel that they are willing to invest right now. You want to accomplish all these things before the end of that call. the end of the call.

The best way to do this, I have found, is to create what's called an "involvement device" and in this, that is the case evaluation. The worst thing you could do in a virtual meeting with a potential is have the person just stare at a screen for 30 minutes, while you barrage them with questions and confuse them with legalese. They need information they can interact with. They need to be able to create the story of their case for you on the video call. Otherwise, they may not be paying attention. They might open a browser tab, or they may be playing Candy Crush on their phone and just nodding along, while you are trying to present to them. At that point, your words are wasted. Another thing to consider, is that as this section of the call progresses, you want the potential to invest more and more in you incrementally. You want to draw them in and get them involved. Again, you want them to paint the picture of their case. You want to get their story and diagram off what they are telling you. You want them to feel like you are already working for them. If you do this right, by creating the story of their case with them , you are giving them all of this information and these diagrams, if they go to another attorney, they are essentially throwing all of that away. If they go with another attorney, after having spent all this time with you, they are going to have to repeat all of this information and people hate to tell their story twice.

Additionally, once you have had this experience with a potential, they are now anchored to you. They associate good feelings with you. It's very hard to separate that out and go with someone else. Even if they do end up trying another attorney, that someone else won't do any of the things you showed the potential in your call. It's going to be a big time let down. So, if that happens, they are still going to come back to you. I realize there are ethical and professional considerations in this. This is a nuanced area you have to get right, and I am going to show you how to do that as well later on.

<<>>

This next part is probably the most important part of the *Virtual Close System*.

An attorney client of mine practices DUI law. He has been with me for a long time. He is a really good attorney. However, there are probably still things he can improve on. We did a mock video call with him and recorded it so we could watch it and provide him with feedback. During his call, he lets the potential know that he can do pretty much everything for them. While it's nice that he offers all this, it is a little bit too accommodating. You have to make the potential work for it a little bit. They will enjoy it more and will be more likely to hire you.

The goal of this call is not to just say, "I can do this for you. I can do that for you. Yes sir. No sir."

Of course, it's not usually that extreme, but what I'm saying is the goal here is to see if the potential qualifies for you to represent them. That is just as important as them wanting to hire you. You don't need to be obnoxious, but it doesn't hurt to say things like,

"I don't take all cases. If your case is a fit for my services, I'll be able to offer you my representation today. One of the things I can do, after you hire me, is I can go to the DMV for you I and then I will also go to the hearings for you," and so on.

However, you should always preface it with something to the effect of, "I don't take all cases. Frankly, I'm very busy so I've got to make sure that all the facts of your case fit. I just want to let you know that. I just want to let you know that right up front."

You have to do that positioning. Play a little bit hard to get but with a valid reason. A lot of attorneys do the opposite of this. They talk about working together and make the potential feel like they are already working with them. If you do this wrong, it pushes the person away and it compromises your authority positioning. It makes it unfortunately paradoxically less likely that a potential is going to hire you even though it feels like what you are saying is helping.

You also have to make sure to ask the potential what the single most important thing is they want to have happen with their case to make it a success. You must ask that question and write down that answer.

Additionally, the fact is you are going to be drawing nearly the same thing on the whiteboard each time you present to a potential client and that's okay. The potential doesn't know that. It will look like it was just done just for them which is true. This is going to create an urge for them to want to reciprocate with you. You did them a big favor. You spent a lot of time and energy on them. You diagrammed out their options. You asked them questions. It's an unbelievably personalized thing to do. The potential is going to feel like, "Wow, this attorney really went all out. I'm going to get back to this guy."

They are going to pay attention to and by doing so, they are going to show respect. They are going to like you.

This will all help you close.

In addition to what you are saying and doing for the client, there are a few other important things to make sure you do during a virtual close call with a potential client. When you go through our *Virtual Close System* modules, you will get to see some of the mock calls we did with our clients. You can see what they did right and what they did wrong. For example, using an HD camera is really important. You want the potential to be able to see you on a clear, crisp camera. A few attorneys dressed too casually. Others were absolutely on point with dress, hair, camera, smile. There are a lot of good techniques you will learn from watching these videos and reading the analysis that goes along with them.

Once you view the mock case evaluations included in the *Virtual Close System* you will see how engaging this process is. You are right there with the attorney. You can see him, hear him and watch their gestures. They ask the potential questions and the potential shares the answers. They diagram the case right there in front of you. Like I mentioned earlier, the potential is building the case with them. It's incredibly engaging for both parties.

At first it may feel awkward but once you get into a routine, it becomes natural. We hear from the attorneys who participated in these mock sessions, that they are using it with their current clients too. Overall, interacting with your clients in this virtual way, is a way to provide better service. The ones that are hip to it, that are taking this to heart and using it, are enjoying their job quite a bit more right now. Frankly, this is going to be a huge competitive advantage for you. Just imagine in your mind just hearing someone's voice versus what I have described to you in our *Virtual Close System.* You don't see them. There is no visual being written down on a whiteboard. You are just being lectured at. Which one do you think is going more compelling? I know from experience now and the attorneys know, it's what I have been telling you about in this book. The methods used in the *Virtual Close System* offer you a massive competitive advantage, when you need it most, which is right now.

Step #3: Presenting Your Offer And Doing It Right

How do you present your fee and service offer so that it looks like it has incredible value in comparison to your competitors? There are several tools that I'm going to talk about that will help you accomplish this. For example, using comparison tables will show all the things that you do, even if they are intangible, compared with what cheaper attorneys can't do. This is a great way for you to put your fees in the right context in front of the potential client. For instance, let's say a competitor has a base rate of $1200, which is lower than your fee. In this case, you can show the potential in the comparison chart what that attorney can't do for them. For example, they don't have the capacity to go to court multiple times. They can't hire expert witnesses. They can't file more than one or two basic motions and on and on and on. The *Virtual Closing System* will teach you how to create these comparison tables that show the potential what they will get if they hire the low fee attorney who does the bare minimum. The same can be done to show the prospective client what they will get if they hire one of the top end firms that charge exorbitant fees.

Then, on the whiteboard, you show the potential where you fall in the middle; from a price standpoint and what they will get when they hire you. You show them why you offer great value, for what you charge. I call this three-level comparison the "sandwich".

This makes a lot of potentials go for you, the middle option because they see the high-priced attorney. They see the super cheap attorney. Then they see, the middle option; the "Goldilocks", the "just right" attorney. Seeing a visual of this reduces the resistance. It makes people more compliant and it makes sense to the brain. Now the potential has even more reasons to retain you. One thing you want to do at this point, as an ace up your sleeve, is to prepare a payment plan option. Keep it hidden for right now. There may be price objections later where it will come in handy.

Step #4: How To Handle Payment

Even though you have the potential convinced they are going to hire you, you aren't done yet. It's not over until the money is in the bank. This is where a lot of deals get lost. Often attorneys think, "Great! They said they want to work with me. I'm going to send them my retainer agreement and we'll get started."

Often, they never hear from the potential again. So again, it's not over until the retainer agreement is signed and you have money.

There are many tools out there that will help you handle retainer. For example, you can pull up DocuSign while you are on the call and get the agreement e-signed digitally right then and there.

However, you still need to make sure this is handled the right way or risk losing the client at this point. With the *Virtual Close System,* you will get the necessary scripts that will help you do it right. For example, you can't just suddenly start reading your retainer agreement to a potential and expect them to pay attention and then get them to immediately sign it. In our system, there are tricks and tips to get you through this process smoothly so that you get that signed agreement. The methods in the VCS will guide you through all the necessary steps to close a potential client; beginning the call, the case evaluation, explaining your fee, getting the retainer signed and getting paid.

Bringing up the fee and payment is probably the scariest moment of any presentation to a potential client.

When you ask, "How do you want to handle payment?", there could be a myriad of different responses. The person could say they don't have money or say they are going think about it, for example. Whatever, it is, there are ways to deal with this. This is again, where scripts come in very handy and the VCS will provide those. You want to be able to elegantly handle this and not get caught off guard. You want to make it seamless and get paid and not lose all this work that you've put in.

Step #5: How Do You Follow Up?

In this last step, we will talk about following up. Again, not everyone is going to say yes on the spot. There is no one on earth that sells 100%. They would be unbelievably wealthy if they did. It just doesn't happen.

Often, no matter how good your meeting with a potential was, some people are still hesitant to commit. They will say they will get back to you or they just can't decide right then and there on the spot. How you follow up with those prospects is critical. It must be done in a professional and ethical way. You can't bother them. The follow up must be done without eroding your positioning; without seeming desperate. The question then is, how do you do this making full use of email, text and phone, and maybe even direct mail?

Choosing only way of follow up is not enough. It's nice for people to hear from you in different ways. You may want to mail the potential something and then text them a few days later. Perhaps you or your admin then calls several days after that. Maybe you check in with the potential client, offering other helpful information related to his or her case. Human nature shows us that most people don't say yes to an offer the first time they see it. They say maybe.

If you follow the advice and methods of the VCS, your closing rate is going to be much higher. The system was designed to do just this. From my days with myduiattorney.org, we had attorneys that couldn't close someone if you stapled the client to them. Others would sign a client maybe 40 to 60 percent of the time. There were superstars and there were people that were just awful when it came to closing a client.

I can even tell you from my own experience, most of the sales we close at Speakeasy Marketing, come from the "maybes" and those potentials who say they are going to think about it. It takes time for some people to say yes. It doesn't matter how good your pitch is; not everyone is going to say yes right on the spot. Every time you meet with a client, you have to do your best to show the potential why they need to invest in you.

To follow up with a potential properly, you have to have a dependable sequence of emails, texts, phone calls, voicemails and direct mail pieces that will be sent. You want to keep yourself at the top of a potential client's mint all times. Remember they are going through their doubts and may even be talking to other attorneys at the same time.

Their family might be telling them, "I don't know if you should do this."

Meanwhile their situation may be worsening.

Of course, there will be potentials that verbally say they want to work with you and will get back to you with the signed retainer agreement. While that's great, that's not a close. How do you get the retainer signed if they just won't do it right then and there? Or even if they have signed a payment plan, you still have to make sure that your fees are coming in.

If you don't have a service to do that for you, you are stuck chasing payment. At the end of this book, I will tell you about the bonus module our VCS includes. There is a company that will get you the entire payment right up front. We also cover what to do if you are doing your own payment plan. How do you make sure you get your money if you are handling this yourself? You have to do the legal work and keep the client engaged and interested and at the same time paying you throughout the case. This becomes too much for an attorney to handle on his or her own.

Lastly, follow up isn't just about getting a client to hire you. It doesn't even end when the client has paid in full or even once the case is over. For example, if you want the client to refer you to others or write a review, guess what? You will need proper follow up procedures. Follow up is an incredibly important part of a successful practice and this is why we cover it in great detail in our VCS.

~~~~~~~~~~~~~~~~~~~~~~~~~~~~~~~~

These are the five things you must get right to close people remotely, to keep your pipeline stuffed and to get through this pandemic successfully and even
~~~~~~~~~~~~~~~~~~~~~~~~~~~~~~~~

continue that success after this is all over. It's not complicated. However, you have to have the right tools. You can't just wing it. You can't just let the receptionist do their thing. That doesn't work anymore. If you do, you will be shooting yourself in the foot and you can't afford to do that now.

You need to follow the 5 steps I will tell you about faithfully. To do that, you need procedures. You need step by step instructions to make sure you are consistent. You, your staff and anyone who answers that phone and who works on the case, needs to take the right steps, in the right order with the right scripts.

Other things that are helpful are props, whiteboards, presentation slides, graphics, price comparison charts and so on. One of my clients even used a breathalyzer in his video case evaluation. He picked it up and showed the prospect while he talked about the specific aspects of their case. It was incredibly engaging. Some areas of law lend themselves to that sort of thing naturally, while some don't. However, that doesn't mean you can't get creative and find different ways to use props regardless of your area of practice.

For example, if you have written a book, you can use that as a prop to show potentials when conversing over the video call. If you have your law diploma, put it up on the wall behind you so the prospective client can see it when you meet online. Use board certifications, family photos, and so on. There are a lot of things you can use to show potentials who you are which will help your conversion.

Additionally, as I mentioned, you will need to use scripts. Again, winging it just doesn't work. Now when interacting with potentials, you don't want to sound like you are reading from a script. However, you have to have one to at least loosely follow; something that you have practiced many times, so you know what you are going to say, and you are comfortable with.

The same goes for your admin staff. They too need to be well rehearsed with scripts and proper training on how to handle incoming calls from potentials. You can't just say to your staff, "Hey, here is a script. Now go make sure you say this all to potential clients."

The *Virtual Closing System* contains everything you need, to get potentials into your virtual office. With the right attitude and the right emotional state, you or your staff can presell them on doing business with you and get them to convert into clients right then and there. Our *Virtual Close System* contains scripts, ideas on what props to use and instructions on all the procedures and resources you will need to put together an amazing presentation to show your potentials. Everything you need to make your client conversion process watertight and super high percentage wise, is included in this system.

The VCS includes training modules for you and your staff, along with two packages.

Before we go any further, I want to say that this may not be the right fit for your practice and that's okay. Our new *Virtual Closing System* is not for every single solo or small firm out there.

It's designed for attorneys who are already getting calls and inquiries. Unfortunately, our *Virtual Closing System* is not going to make your phone ring. However, what it will do, is it will guide you through how to handle incoming potentials in the best way possible. It's used for conversion. Again, if you are not getting phone calls right now, it isn't going to change that. However, even if that is the case, the VCS can still prepare you for how to close leads when they do come flooding back; once the economy comes back and pandemic is behind us. You will already be well equipped to handle new ways to close potentials and have that competitive advantage over your competitors.

CHAPTER 5

GOLD VIRTUAL CLOSING SYSTEM

The first system I want to tell you about is the *Gold Virtual Close System which* includes five different modules. The first module includes scripts that will guide you and your staff on how to properly answer and handle incoming calls from potentials, as well as other types of inquiries including emails, Live Chat inquiries and so on. Module one also covers screening out price-shoppers and establishing your positioning.

We will show you how to pre-sell potentials even before initial consult begins.

In module two you will learn how to conduct a case evaluation through video or screenshare. We will talk about how to build rapport and trust with a potential client and how to engage the person by walking them through their own case. When done right, this makes it almost impossible for a potential client to leave the session and not hire you.

In the third module we show you how to present your service package and fees to the potential – to make your services perceived as more valuable versus the competitors. Module four is focused on how to walk the potential through your retainer agreement through the video session or though screen-share.

In module five (Platinum Package Only) we will show you the proper way to follow up with potentials who say "maybe", using time-spaced and custom-messaging email, text, phone and direct mail.

Overview of the Modules

Module #1: Who Is Answering The Phone?

In Module 1 of the *Virtual Close System*, you will find scripts for every person that could possibly answer your phone including an answering service, your admin, you, your law partner, etcetera. I talk about what's wrong with how law firms are answering their phones. Why do I talk about it? Because I know it will help you identify those same things in your own office and figure out how to instead, do them the right way. I show you how to precondition prospects to retain you versus your competitors. I'm going to explain to you how to gather information and strengthen your positioning and how to transition the potential onto the video call. There are nuances that have to be overcome when you can't set up a traditional office visit. It's not just like you just answer the phone and right away go to video. Again, there are scripts within the *Virtual Close System* that will guide through these processes. There is a script to use if it's not you who answers the phone, but rather your admin or other staff. There is a script they can use if you are not available to take the call; if you are in court, if you are out of the office, or on another call. There is even a script for when the incoming call has to go to voicemail. Scripts are everything.

Module #2: How Do You Do Case Evaluation?

Module 2 is the most exciting module. Here we show you how to conduct the case evaluation. We even have included critiques that you can check out that will help you. We show you how to set the stage; how to start the call and once you are on video, how you keep it flowing, building up the pace and how to engage the potential and create interest and excitement. We also cover how to overcome early price objections. In this module you will learn how to keep control of the call and defend your price early on by using scripts. Again, if someone is asking early, its usually a sign of trouble. It doesn't mean that they are a bad client, but you have to be able to defer that in a nice way and keep them going because otherwise you can lose them right then and there.

Module #3: How Do You Ask For The Sale?

In Module 3 we will go over how to ask for the sale. How do you ask that scary question, "Would you like to get started?"

Again, objections can come up at this point. In this module we go over how you handle those. We show you how to explain to the potential what their case could look like if they act now versus waiting to hire an attorney.

For every type of case or area of the law, there are ways to show the potential client what potential outcomes their case could have and what it could look like along the way based on when they act to hire you. So, when people have objections, you can tell them, "You don't have to decide right now, but I wouldn't wait any longer than two weeks."

That's important. You want to also give them a reason to act now and that's part of what I just talked about with future pacing. If they have objections, you can be prepared. What you don't want to happen, is to hear an objection that you've never heard before and not have an answer ready.

Module #4: How Do You Go Through Retainer Agreement The Right Way Right Then And There And Get The Payment?

In Module 4, we cover what to do once you have the yes from the potential. They have decided they want to work with you. This is the home stretch, which is why you certainly don't want to trip and fall at this point.

So, how do you go through the retainer agreement the right way, right then and there? How do you get that payment? Retainer agreements are wonderful but at this point, the potential client can still slip away from you. You don't want to be stuck representing someone with no payment. How do you pour cement on the deal to finalize it? Then you want to set expectations on what it's going to be like working together. You want to lay the ground now, for positive reviews and referrals later.

In summary, with Gold package, you receive:

- Qualifying
- Evaluating
- Presenting
- Closing potentials

CHAPTER 6

PLATINUM VIRTUAL CLOSING SYSTEM

Module #5: How Do You Follow Up With The Maybes?

Module 5 is exclusive to our Platinum package and here we focus on following up with the "maybes". A lot of attorneys don't want to handle this part themselves. Maybe they don't know how to do it without feeling squeamish. In Module 5 of the *Virtual Closing System* I'm going to teach you how. We have systems in place where we get the potentials from you which you haven't yet converted. We then will do the follow up emails, texts, phone calls, voicemails and so on. This is all handled in a professional and ethical manner and will help you get those people back.

Having the proper follow up protocol is an art. There is a lot that goes into it. Do you send an email day one, a phone call day two and direct mail day three? Do you send emails on days one, five, nine and 11 and intersperse them with two phone calls? You do not want to erode your positioning. What you say, when you say it and how to say it, is all included in the *Virtual Closing System*'s Platinum package in Module 5 for you.

You want to chase these people in the right way; professionally and ethically. You must maintain your positioning and still grab those potentials that "got away". They are the icing on the cake, more money in your account. Those extra clients who, before using the follow up techniques I will share with you would have gotten away, are more stability in this economic environment. There is no reason not to do it.

CHAPTER 7

MODULE #1: QUALIFY

In this module we will cover the answering the phone when a prospect calls, authority positioning, the preconditioning of your prospect and the transition to video calling on Zoom.

The first question is, who answers your phone? Is it your admin? Is it an answering service? If so, we have the scripts for those scenarios. Are you, the attorney, answering the calls that come in? In some solo and small practices, the attorney themselves have to do so. There is nothing wrong with that. We have a specific script for you as well.

We also help you prepare for when your phone has to go to voicemail, which is also important. I've called plenty of law firms where there is no voicemail set up or the phone number doesn't work. I recommend you check your law office phone number at least once a month to make sure it is working properly and that calls are being directed to the proper place and callers are receiving appropriate messaging. You might have potential calls that may be going into the abyss and you don't even know it.

There might be people calling your office after hours. You don't want to miss those calls. Nowadays there inexpensive answering services you can hire that will answer your phones overnight and on weekends. Your phone always needs to be answered. In this day and age, you can't afford to lose any potentials.

If your calls absolutely have to go to voicemail, you need to ensure the messaging is good and that calls are returned as soon as possible.

We've called many law firms and the most common thing we hear when someone picks up is a generic, "Law Office."

Then when you ask for the attorney, all too often the person who answered the phone just says that he or she is not in and directs us to call back later or says they will take a message. Basically, if whoever answers your phone is treating a prospect as an inconvenience or essentially telling them to go away, guess what they are going to do?

They already have their smartphone in hand or are on their laptop. Once they hang up with your office, all they have to do is Google and keep searching for the next guy who will take their call.

Periodically we do audits of various attorneys in different practice areas. We build a list of 100 or so attorneys and call their offices and inquire about a specific legal problem. Approximately 70 offices usually don't answer the phone, while 30 or so will answer but the attorney isn't there. With the remaining offices we call, we usually get through to an attorney or two and even talk with him or her. Out of approximately 100 total offices that we call, we generally come out with maybe one or two attorneys that are good prospects consider working with. This is for every area of law; divorce, auto accidents, estate planning and so on. The numbers that we see from these periodic audits are awful.

If these numbers tell us anything, is it any wonder why so many attorneys have problems getting new business? Unfortunately, this is just the plain truth. We have seen it.

Another problem we come across in our audits, is how the phone is answered and how the conversation progresses between the potential and whoever took the call. There is often no information capture. The callers are not being asked their name, phone number, email address and so on. You can't be shy. Whoever has the first contact with a potential has to get the key details. If you don't, once the caller is off the phone, you will probably never hear from them again. They are not calling you back. They are just going to keep dialing. That is what most prospects will do.

Get this information so you can contact these people again. Once you have an email address, a phone number, a mailing address or whatever it is, you can follow up. If you miss capturing a potential's contact information, your marketing dollars are just going down the drain. You are missing out on hundreds of thousands of dollars a year in opportunities.

Often when people call an attorney's office, they are intimidated. Most times when someone needs a lawyer, they aren't a great time in their life. Someone has died or someone is contesting a will. Maybe it's someone who is divorcing or was in a car accident. Maybe it's someone who is facing criminal charges. Generally, potentials aren't in a good mindset. When people are calling your office, they may be upset or scared. They don't want to be talking to you.

Unfortunately, even if you get a client a positive result in their case, they will associate you with a negative experience in their life. They might be happy for a day or two. They are relieved. They might love you after you were able to get a great result. However, regardless of that, they probably hope they never hear from you again. It's not you. It's because you were unfortunately there at a horrible time in their life. They don't want to remember it. This is the sad state of affairs with being an attorney. You do noble things and you make a lot of people's lives better. Thank God for you. However, unfortunately this is just the reality. What I am getting at here, is one of the last things that I want to address when it comes to phone etiquette and protocol when potentials call your office. How law firms answer their phone is critical when it comes to empathy. Often, there is no emotional connection. There is no rapport. There is no understanding of the caller's emotions and how to deal with them.

Remember, the people are calling your office may be nervous. They are intimidated and possibly upset. They are stressed and are not thinking clearly. You have to acknowledge those emotions when you hear from them. It goes a long way. Potentials, of course, want a professional who is capable and knowledgeable. However, they also want and need someone who actually cares about them. They want some degree of empathy. If you are stone cold and there is no emotional connection, there is no reason for that person to hire you.

I can tell you, I personally don't want to work with people who are rude or are completely turned off emotionally. I don't want to hire someone who doesn't really care about me and you don't either. So, don't go that route. It doesn't represent you well.

~~~~~~~~~~~~~~~~~~~~~~~~~~~~~~~~

The next point I want to address in the first module is pre-conditioning prospects to retain you versus everyone else they have called. Sometimes you are the first call. Other times you are the tenth call. How are you going to make this person remember you? How are you going to get this potential to say,
~~~~~~~~~~~~~~~~~~~~~~~~~~~~~~~~

"Yes. Let's go forward and let's talk about my case," instead of, "Let me think about it. I'll get back to you."

You don't want to hear that. So how do you precondition potentials? First, you need to give them a good experience on the phone. Like I mentioned previously, there are many ways to do this right.

Even if a prospective client doesn't hire you, it's okay. It doesn't mean you won't still get the case. If you have made a good first impression, they may remember you and come back. However, without a good first experience, they are never going to call you back and may even write a bad review. People want to be understood. They don't want to be blown off. By doing this right from the start, you are preconditioning the potential to like you. Someone who likes you, gets to know you and trusts you will want to do business with you.

You hear my podcasts. You get my emails. You may have even spoken to me on the phone. We've been marketing to you for years. If I didn't do that you wouldn't have purchased this training. The same goes for you. I'm not telling you anything that we don't do. I'm not telling you anything that we haven't learned. These methods work.

You need to give prospects a unique and interesting experience with you. Don't talk to them in a monotone voice, speaking only legalese and avoid getting into anything emotional. That will only lead to a negative, or at best, an unimpressionable experience for the potential. Again, let them know they are understood and are being heard. Before they even sign with you, give them some insight into what might happen in their case. Provide an experience where they are engaged that makes them want to work with you and makes you really stand out.

Finally, if you don't try and if you don't work at it, you are just going to be a run of the mill call for a potential. They are going to forget you two seconds after they hang up the phone. I know you want to be professional and ethical. You want to demonstrate your experience, be authoritative and appear prestigious and knowledgeable. However, you want, in summation to be the, "I have got to hire this attorney" experience.

When you accomplish this, you can precondition prospects to pay the prices that you want, be better behaved as clients, and not question everything you do. They will have trust and faith and overall, you will both have a better attorney-client better client experience. You will be happy to represent them and they won't be an albatross around your neck.

~~~~~~~~~~~~~~~~~~~~~~~~~~~~~~~~~~

In this next section, we are going to go into the scripts. As I mentioned earlier, do not forget to gather as much relevant information as you can from the prospect. I don't care if the person doesn't appear to be the right client for you. In the beginning, train your staff, yourself and anyone that touches that phone to gather details from the prospective client no matter what. You may need it later. For example, it isn't uncommon for a potential to come off as a tire kicker
~~~~~~~~~~~~~~~~~~~~~~~~~~~~~~~~~~

or perhaps, at first, they might not seem serious about hiring you. Then suddenly something that was said to them during that initial call turns them and now they want to do business with you. If you didn't get all those important details before, you could be out of luck. Additionally, if you have that contact information you can also be doing follow up with them in the meantime. Imagine if I marketed to you once and you never heard from me again. I would have starved to death long ago.

I also want you to make sure you are building your authority positioning or have it built for you. It's going to make your job that much easier if you do. For example, when a call is transferred to you, whoever is passing the potential to you, has hopefully laid the groundwork. They should have preconditioned the caller and built your authority before you even speak to the person. You also need to make sure when they hand off a call to you, it is done in a warm manner and not just a cold transfer, dropping the potential into a call with you, who at that point is a stranger. Additionally, you should always leave a path open to call the prospect back in case you can't do everything right then and there.

Scripts For Module 1:

In this next section we are going to go over the scripts I have been telling you about.

For anyone who is answering the phone in your office, who is not you, (this could include an answering service, admin, other staff, etc.) there are scripts that will help them execute the preconditioning and positioning.

First, we are going to go through the script for when you, the attorney, answer the phone. Again, the goal is to position you as the expert, so you retain a much higher percentage of better behaved, less price resistant clients.

You: "Law Office of ABC, this is John Smith. Are you calling about a legal matter?"

Obviously, if the person says no, you dispatch with them as you need to. If they say yes, then you say:

You: "Very good. I'm attorney Smith. Let me get my notepad. I want to make some notes while I ask you about your situation. Just give me a moment."

The caller describes their legal issue. At some point you say:

You: "I'm sorry to hear that you are going through this."

Remember, show some empathy, and don't grill the potential as if they are on the stand. Right away, it is important to start building rapport.

You: "Okay. I understand you so far and I do have some questions. Before I go on though, I want to ask you one important question. What would you say is the single most important issue that you are facing that you absolutely want resolved above all else if possible?"

The person will tell you and, again, you write this down. This is important because this information will be used in the follow up later or you will bring this up later on in the call. You want to show the person he or she is being listened to.

You: "Based on what you've told me about your situation, I'm confident that I can help you. I say this because I've handled several hundred cases that are very similar to yours. I don't have a perfect track record, but I have good results for a significant number of clients in your situation. I also want to let you know that I do have a large case load and, my representation is not the cheapest. I focus on complex and difficult cases like yours. I have X number of years of experience, with over a hundred cases that sound very similar to yours. I often can get good outcomes."

Let the person take in that information. At this point, there is a branch in the script. If you haven't done a Speak a Book with us (we offer that at Jacobs & Whitehall), continue as normal. However, if you have written a book through Speak a Book, there is a little bit extra for you in the script.

You: One last thing, before we go deeper into your situation, I wanted to mention that I recently wrote a book on (your practice area). Instead of having you buy it off Amazon, I'm happy to send you a complimentary copy through email or by mail. It has a lot of relevant information that I think will be useful to your case. It will help you with your situation whether we work together or not. What's your best email address to send that to? I'll have it sent out to you right now."

As soon as you have their email address or mailing address, make sure you send that to your admin and have someone send the book by PDF or even better, by PDF and physical mail that same day. Don't wait. Even if the client ends up retaining you, still send it at least to their email address, if not their physical mail. It will help keep that client happy if they retained you. And of course, if they haven't retained you, it's a very important follow up tool.

Script For Admins, Secretaries, Answering Services And Other Staff

This next script is the script for admins, secretaries, answering services and other staff who are answering your phone.

Again, the goal here is to position you as an authority so you can get better behaved, less price resistant prospects.

Admin: "Law office of John Smith. This is Susan. Are you calling about a legal matter?"

The prospect answers.

Admin: "No problem. I'm going to ask you a bit about your situation and take some notes, if that's ok. Okay. Let me get my pen. Tell me a little bit about your legal matter so I can match you with the right attorney.

The caller states their legal issue and again, same thing, the person who answered the phone should show empathy.

Admin: "I'm sorry that you are going through this."

The admin or whoever answers the phone should not sound robotic. They must be personable.

Admin: By the way, what's the single most important issue you are facing that you feel absolutely has to be resolved above all else? I'm going to let the attorney know about it.

Again, capture the information and write it down so it can be used for follow-up if necessary.

Admin: Based on what you have told me about your situation, I'm going to connect you with Attorney John Smith. He has handled several hundred cases that are very similar to yours and he is very knowledgeable. He is very busy and frankly, his representation is not the lowest cost out there because he does only focus on complex and difficult cases. He does have a lot of specific expertise on cases that are pretty similar to yours, from what it sounds like."

Again, if you haven't written a Speak a Book, the admin would continue as below.

Admin: "Hold on for a moment, let me get her on the phone."

If you have written a Speak a Book, you can add this to your script:

Admin: "One last thing, before I transfer you. Attorney Smith has recently written a book on (practice area). Instead of having you buy it on Amazon, he wanted me to make it available to people who call and have serious issues like you, for free. What's your best email address? Let me get a copy out to you right away. Okay, please hold on for a minute. Let me get him on the phone right now."

Then, your admin should connect you with the potential on the line, with an introduction. Do not let them patch the potential through with no transition.

Admin: Hi Attorney Smith. It's Susan from the front desk. I have Tom Jones on the phone. He is calling about a (practice area) issue. Based on what he has told me, I thought you'd be the best person for him to speak to about his case."

Attorney: "Hi Tom. I'll be glad to talk to you. Thanks Susan, I'll take it from here."

That's a warm transfer. You have been pre-positioned. The person has been preconditioned and you are much more likely to have a better call.

~~~~~~~~~~~~~~~~~~~~~~~~~~~~

In this next section we are going to talk about getting the prospect to transition to video. At this point, someone has answered the phone and spoke to the prospect and then warm transferred them over to you.

The goal of this next script is to give this potential a solid reason to join you on a video call. You can't just say, "Hey. Let's do a video call!" because some people aren't naturally comfortable with that. You have to give them a reason.
~~~~~~~~~~~~~~~~~~~~~~~~~~~~

Attorney: "Tom, just to let you know, the best way I've found to help my clients, is to do a case evaluation together on a video conference call. Let me explain what's involved. I'm going to email you or text you a link right now to join me on video conferencing. The service I use is called Zoom and together we will diagram your case out. We are going to show the facts, the backgrounds, the parties involved and so on. It's a super useful way to help visualize your case and show you some scenarios of what may happen. When we are done, I'm going to send you a copy of this little case eval which will be very useful for you, even if you end up retaining another attorney. It's going to put you light years ahead in your case. So, it's super useful. Don't worry, this case eval and the initial consult we are doing are free of charge. On the video call, you'll be able to see me and I can share my screen, so we can literally work on this case eval together. Let me send you the link. Did you get it? Okay, great. Please join me now on the video call and when I see you in there, I'm going to look and see if your microphone is enabled. Then once we are set, we are going to hang up on the phone and just stay in the video conference because that will be launched simultaneously."

~~~~~~~~~~~~~~~~~~~~~~~~~~~~~~

Here is a sample script.

Voicemail: "You've reached ABC Law Office. We guarantee to return your call, text or email within 12 hours, even on weekends and nights. Our attorney, John Smith, has handled hundreds (practice area) cases and prioritizes having good relations with his clients. If you have a legal issue, either leave a voicemail message with your name, email and phone number or text us your name, email and phone number or go to www.ABClawoffice.com and click the contact form. Whatever is easiest for you. Again, give us your name, email and phone number and if you can, a time to call you back. Again, we promise, within 12 hours, we will contact you back, possibly sooner. Thank you for calling."

Now, compare that to whatever script you have or don't have right now. This one is a lot better. The potential is going to see you are taking this seriously. I
~~~~~~~~~~~~~~~~~~~~~~~~~~~~~~

can't tell you how many places we've called where the voicemail says, "The voicemail you are calling has not been setup," or it just says to leave a message. Please don't let this be you.

~~~~~~~~~~~~~~~~~~~~~~~~~~~~~~~~~~

Here is another bonus script for when you, the attorney, is not available or is out of the office, and can't take the call right away.

Person Answering Phone: "Hi. This is ABC Law Office. My name is Mary. Are you calling because you are facing a legal issue?"

Caller: "Yes, I am. (They may describe the issue or not)

Person Answering Phone: "I want to make sure you are matched with the right attorney who has experience with your type of situation. So, I just want to ask a few questions to help me match you. What's your full name, phone number and your email?"
~~~~~~~~~~~~~~~~~~~~~~~~~~~~~~~~~~

Get that first because if, for whatever reason, you need to contact this person back, you can. You can also use that information to remarket to them.

Caller: (The person gives answers or person may say) "I don't want to give that information. I just want to talk to an attorney."

If they do that which is rare, the admin or other staff can say:

Person Answering Phone: I'd be glad to help you, but I do need that information so that I can route you properly. If I don't have that, I can't patch you on to an attorney. I'm sorry. We are very busy."

You might not get much information in this situation. However, you should at least push back and press for it a little bit. Don't let those people through, assuming they have a legal issue.

Assuming they did give your admin an answer with their name, email and phone number, they should have written it down and passed it on to you.

Make a template that is easily accessible to whoever is answering the phone:

- **Name of Caller:**
- **Time they called:**
- **Phone number:**
- **Email address:**
- **Practice Area:**

Person Answering Phone: "Great. Thank you for that information. I just have two more questions. One, can you tell me briefly, your story about what happened to cause this situation?"

That is showing empathy. Ideally, the caller will give a few facts. Keep it brief, maybe 5 minutes. Write down some notes and then the admin should say:

Person Answering Phone: Okay, I just have one last question. What is the single most important result that you want to get from your case? Please be specific.

I'm asking you because I want to let the attorney know what to focus on when they talk to you."

There is nothing wrong with asking this question. This is an immensely powerful question because it opens the door for you getting back to that person. We'll go into that later in another module, but this is a really important because it shows you where that person's mind is at. If it's divorce, they may say custody of the children is the most important thing right now. If it's an auto accident, it may mean getting their car fixed. If it's estate planning, it may be that the person's father is in hospice. You want to pull this information out of the person as soon as you can. That's why we ask it and always give a reason why you are asking.

Person Answering Phone: Thank you. First, I'm sorry to hear that you are having this trouble. The attorney that has handled hundreds of these cases that sound pretty similar to yours, is attorney John Smith. Even though he is in court right now, he does have a couple of open appointment times. One is today at 3:00

or tomorrow at 2:00 or tomorrow at 4:00. What's the best time for you and I'll schedule you?"

You don't ever want the person who is answering your phone to just say you aren't there or are busy. They need to give specific appointment times that are available. At the beginning of each day, tell whoever answers your phone, the times you are free. It might not be perfect, or your schedule may change, but if you give your staff something to go off of, it will help tremendously.

Make sure the person who is answering your phone, doesn't just give the potential client an easy out and tell them to call back. They should at least try to schedule an appointment.

Person Answering the Phone: "Okay, great. I'm going to email you a reminder now and I'm going to text you as well. Just so, you know, I think you are going to get a lot out of talking with Attorney John Smith. He has many clients who have given him positive reviews and who were very happy with his representation."

Again, that's another positioning statement that will help.

Now, you have the person's name, email and phone number and likely a specific time when they will meet with you. You are in a much better place than just allowing your staff to answer the phone, "Law office. He's not here."

These scripts are designed to help you, but you have to use them. If your admin, other staff or your answering service say they don't want to use scripts, I would highly consider either giving them a strict talking to or letting them go. This is your business and your money. I don't want you to lose thousands of dollars in client revenue every month because someone on your team just doesn't want to do what needs to be done.

You should demand it from your people. There is nothing wrong with it. It's not going to hurt them. It's just a script. As soon as you implement this into your office strategies, you will see how much of an uptick there is in your business.

~~~~~~~~~~~~~~~~~~~~~~~~~~~

Dealing With Potentials Who Are Shy And Don't Want To Get On Video

You may get some resistance from potentials when transitioning them from an initial phone call to a video session. Some people are shy or don't like to be on camera. We have come up with a simple solution to this. We suggest to the attorneys to tell their potentials who might be hesitant to do a video session that, "Hey. You know what? I'm going to be the one presenting doing the whiteboard session with you and going over your case. I need to be on video, while I present your options, but you really don't have to turn on your camera, if you aren't comfortable. Just keep your audio on. Once I turn on my video, let me know when you can see me. I will make sure I can hear you and vice versa. We can do this consult just as you would, but now you will get the added benefit of seeing me, and
~~~~~~~~~~~~~~~~~~~~~~~~~~~

we can still diagram out your case on the whiteboard together. Is that ok?".

The attorneys we have talked to have told us they have never had someone say no when they frame it that way.

CHAPTER 8

MODULE #2: EVALUATE

At this point, you have successfully preconditioned the client, you and you have them on the phone. You have asked them to transfer to video conferencing. They have agreed and now you are about to start the video conference.

As attorneys, you have been doing consults by phone for many years. I'm not here to tell you how to do your consultation with a potential. You know how to do that with your eyes closed. I am here, however, to give you ways to augment, improve and condition it specifically for video. There are a lot of things you can do to enhance this experience for your potential clients. By doing so, you will also make the time a lot more effective for you and make it easier to convert the potentials.

In Module 2, we show you how to gather information and build rapport. We teach you how to use an involvement device in your video case eval, while engaging the client, with the ultimate goal, of course, of asking for the sale. Those are the things you want to do. Build rapport, do the case eval, gather info and ask for that sale.

Setting The Stage

As you start to do the video consults you will find little changes you will want to make along the way to better your presentation. It might be something as simple as going from headphones with a cord to going wireless. You might notice certain angles where the sunlight comes in or the overhead light makes your coloring off and so on.

I definitely recommend doing a few mock video calls so you can see what your potentials will see. Get comfortable with your surroundings so everything appears natural.

Remember when are going to talk to the potential, they are preconditioned to work with you if you've used the scripts. You need to maintain that positioning as you continue to talk to the potential. Visual cues are incredibly important to use to your advantage. For example, there are deliberate props you may want to use such as awards or diplomas that may appear behind you on the wall. If you have done a Speak a Book, you might want to set it on your desk facing the camera. There's nothing wrong with these tactics. They are visual cues. You don't have to say anything, but they convey authority. This is very important. You may even want to have a previous case eval on the whiteboard behind you. You could make it a shill type thing and say, "Let me erase this and we can get started. I was just getting done with someone."

A clean whiteboard is a clean start. Even the fact of having the board and you wiping it down indicates to the potential, "Okay. We are ready to begin."

Another visual cue or prop you might consider is having a big stack of files on your desk. You could let the client know, "As you can see, I am pretty busy. These are the whole stack of files that I'm working on. I'm glad you called when you did because I do have time for one or two more cases this month."

All of these visual cues are not meant to be deceptive. They influence how a person thinks and how they're going to perceive you and on average, that's very important. So, you want to appear neat on camera. You don't want to be dressed sloppy or have messy hair, obviously but you don't have to go crazy.

It's not like a job interview where you're perfectly manicured. People understand that you're in a remote environment. Personal items, such as a family picture, are humanizing things. They're actually very good and if you're strategic about it, they can really help you get the prospect and convert them. You would be very surprised. You can even setup deliberate interruptions that serve your purpose.

For example, if you're in an office setting, you may want to have your admin come in and ask you something. You just turn to the admin and say, "I have got about 15 minutes left here. Tell Mr. Smith I'll get right back to him."

Then apologize to your potential for the interruption and go on with the case eval. You can create a little bit of urgency or the appearance of being busy. Again, take this as you will. If you feel it is deceptive, don't do it. However, if it is done the right way it's not going to hurt anybody, and it could help you. On the other hand, you want to keep unplanned interruptions at bay for sure. People coming in and disturbing you is not good unless you're controlling what's happening.

Let your admin and other staff know not to interrupt you. Let the potential client know, "Just so you know, my phone is on silent. I've asked my staff not to come in for the next 30 minutes. I'm all yours."

All these things provide reassuring environmental type cues that will help your conversion.

Next, I want to cover the call with the potential. Your environment is set. You know what you're going to show and say. You know how your case eval outline is going to look basically and the steps you'll take to go through it.

When you are transferring into the video call, remember, you have three jobs. One, is to maintain your positioning as an authority. Hopefully, you've used the scripts and had whoever answers the phone, to position you so you're not going in cold. This will make your job a lot easier. Remember again, maintain your position as an authority.

Like I said, that case eval is incredibly important. You want to get the potential involved. Don't lecture to the person; get them engaged. Have them help you draw the case out. Ask questions. Pause for a second and say, "What do you think about this right here? What should we put here?" and that kind of thing.

You want to demonstrate expertise, but you also want to keep them participating.

You ask, "What's your full name?", and then you write it down.

"What's your wife or husband's name?" and you again, write it down.

"You said you have three kids. OK."

You draw three circles, and so on.

"You were going eastbound. I'm going to draw your car here and the police, how far were they behind you?"

Again, keep the potential involved the whole time in making this picture of their case. Build rapport. Don't interrogate them. Be human. You're on camera so smile a little bit. Show confidence but don't be stone cold. Talk to this person. Ask them how they are doing. Look up at them periodically.

Those are your three jobs; maintain positioning, involve the person and build rapport so that you can ask for the sale.

Putting people at ease is important, especially in the very beginning. You want to give the potential an approximate timeframe of how long you will be talking.

You might say something like, "Just so you know, these consults, usually they go 20 to 30 minutes. We don't usually need to go longer than that. If you need me to go a little faster than that, we might have to reschedule, or we could try to do this quickly in maybe 15 minutes minimum."

Let them know upfront what to expect. Tell the potential what you are going to talk about and that you might have some questions for them along the way. Let them know you are going to be drawing on the whiteboard.

And let them know, "If at any time you can't see me on the camera or important things I'm writing out on the whiteboard, just let me know. I want to make sure that you get something out of this."

Be a human being. Give the potential the lay of the land and get them comfortable. It just makes people feel better.

Then continue to walk them through the rest of the call.

"Like I said, we will do the case eval. I'm going to do all the writing. You're going to listen and give me the details of the case. Then when we are done, I will send you this case eval by email. At the end of the call, I'll ask you what you'd like to do from here."

You're preparing the potential early on that you're going to ask if they want to work with you or not, which is good to do. I would also add at the end of the call, "I'm going to have some homework for you because there are a few additional questions. There are some things I will need to look into a littler deeper and I will need some documents from you after this."

Generally, you aren't going to capture every piece of information you need in that initial call. It's usually not possible.

Tell the potential, "I find that I get the best results when my clients work with me and give me what I need quickly. So, I'll have a little bit of homework. It won't be too onerous, but just to let you know that's what I have for you at the end. I'm going to give you periodic reminders as we go. Remember, our calls are typically 30 minutes. I'm going to tell you when we're at the halfway mark and when we're near the end just so you can keep a sense of time."

Remember your job is to put the person at ease. Tell them what's coming next and you'll have a pretty smooth call.

The last thing I want to talk about in this section are early price issues and controlling the call.

Some of this may be obvious to most of you, while some of it might be a surprise.

If someone asks you about price right up front, it doesn't necessarily mean that they're a bad client. Some people are just prone to bring it up right up front. You may even get that question multiple times throughout the call.

I'm going to provide you with a mini script on how to handle these price questions. Until you have the opportunity to present, do the case eval and really build rapport, answering pricing questions is only going to lead to problems. The potential hasn't experienced you yet. They haven't formed enough of an impression to respect you to move forward. Some people are so cut and dry that it works if price questions are asked and answered up front. However, if someone is not willing to wait 15 or 20 minutes and go through that intake with you, and they are bringing it up multiple times, if you can't defer them, then you've just got to let them go. They just are not in the state of mind where they're going to listen to you right then or they're not controllable. If you can't control a client when you're at the initial consult stage, good luck controlling them once they hire you, if they do. They are going to be a pain and you don't want that.

On the other hand, how do you defer a price? We are going to go over other price issues and how to handle them. Here I want to talk about the price deferral script.

Potential Client: "How much do you charge for representation?", or "I already spoke to somebody and they quoted me $1000. How much do you charge?"

These are not the things you want to hear. Some are smoke screens. The potential may be willing to pay you, but they don't trust you yet. They don't know. However, some of these may be valid. The only way to find out, though, is to really challenge them a bit. When they say these things to you, here's what you can say:

You: "Listen, I'm not trying to be slick with you. However, when people ask me how much I charge, I honestly have to tell them it does depend on the complexity of their case. But let me give you a quick example. How much does a car cost? If you want a 600 series Mercedes that performs like a dream, it's going to be $150,000. If you want an old junker that has 100,000 miles, it'll be far cheaper. The same goes with attorneys. So, for me, there are two levels of pricing. You may have a super complex case. Maybe you will need multiple court appearances, expert witnesses, accounting services or other professionals in addition to my legal services. If you absolutely must have a great outcome in your case because your freedom is on the line or maybe you are in the military or have a commercial driver's license, for example, that costs between $15,000 to $30,000.

On the other hand, if your case is simple, or if you only want the bare minimum of legal help, then the cheapest low-level lawyers I know charge $1000 to $1500 for these kinds of cases. Keep in mind though, with everything in life, you get what you pay for.

The good news is that I'm nowhere near the most expensive, but I'm also not the cheapest. So, I've got a quick question for you now. On a scale 1 to 10, 10 being the most expensive, the most work and one being barely any legal work is involved, where do you think your case is going to fall?"

The potential client will give you a number.

You: "OK, great. Well, let's go over your case and then we can see where you're likely going to end up. Even if we don't end up working together, at least you'll have a much clearer idea of what representation may cost you and why."

That's the price deferral script. If you do this right, they will be quiet, and they will go through the call with you. If you handle this wrong, it's very likely the potential could just go away or they may just say, "I just can't afford it."

In this case, at least you're giving them a high and a low and you're the potential right off the bat where you fall. They will most likely feel a bit better and you are kind of homing in on a price range without giving them a number. It sort of puts the power back in your hands. If they ask you again about your pricing, as you do the intake, just remind him or her of this.

You: "Listen, on a scale of 1 to 10, you are coming in at about a four. We're getting close to the answer. I need about five to 10 more minutes to get you there. Is that fair?"

If someone gives you a one, you probably don't want to take the case anyway. If someone tells you it's 10, then you may start salivating. Either way you need to ask the potential client that question. Again, it puts the power back in your hands.

Now, let's break down the module. The first thing is the case eval or the involvement device. I've learned quite a bit from speaking to various attorneys about seeing what works best.

What do you want to identify? First, this needs to be a templated process. You don't want to just shoot from the hip or have to reinvent the wheel every time you work with a potential.

Let's take divorce, for example. You may want do templates for all different scenarios. Do you cover divorce with children? High net-worth divorces? Long-term marriages? For criminal law, you may want to create templates for drug cases, DUI, sex cases and so on. For personal injury you may want to have templates for auto accidents, auto wrecks with no significant bodily injury versus death and so on. There are a lot of ways to slice every single practice area.

Next, let's talk about what the case evaluation should look like. Depending on the practice area, the process will differ.

Let's take personal injury auto accident cases as an example. You will first want to diagram the scene of the accident. Ask the potential things like, "Where was your car? Were you going north or south, east or west?".

Then draw the street and car.

Then ask, "What happened? Where were you hit? Where were the bystanders? Did you crash on to anything?".

You draw a diagram of the scene as best as the potential can remember. This helps jog their memory. It will help answer a lot of questions you may have. It could tell you whether this person even has a case or not.

For family law issues, you will want to do a family tree. That's your diagram. Draw the potential and their age with a circle. Then draw the spouse the same way. Draw a line between the two and indicate the length of the marriage. Then you want to include the children. Are they from the potential's marriage?

Are they from a previous marriage? For a previous marriage, you may want to use a dashed line going to the previous spouse or partner. You want to construct a family tree diagram like that. This shows the possible associations or other people who might be involved in the case such as mothers, brothers, uncles, cousins, grandparents; other people who could have rights or other complicated matters. Then you want to draw out the assets and indicate if the house, for example, is in both names? Is the potential in a community property state? Does the wife have a collection of old coins? Does the husband have a motorcycle? Do they have assets from before the marriage? You will want to do a diagram of both parties in the marriage; before the marriage, what they had separately and what they have together. You may want to draw vertical dotted lines and have a timeline associated with all this information. I'm being not too prescriptive here because this is your bailiwick; this is what you are good at. I just want to reaffirm that a diagram and timeline is critical for any case eval, showing major events. The timeline could be either at the bottom of the diagram or on its own separate page. Another element that is going to be critical is the timeline going forward; the potential things that could happen. This is probably best represented by a tree structure, a branching tree. That would be a new page. The top of the tree is where the client is at and then the branches are the major decision points. Along each branch, you could write the anticipated timeline. Another critical element to this case eval would be a sheet of basic facts.

For criminal defense, I will use an arrest situation as an example. For this potential you will want to ask him or her what the events were before, leading up to the arrest. That's part of the timeline. Then you will want to ask what happened during the arrest and through the incarceration and release. You might ask, "Were you released on your own recognizance or on bail? And what has happened since?".

That timeline is a bit more complicated and segmented, but it has those three parts at least to it. Then, of course, very importantly, is the future timeline with the branching possibilities.

You might want to use the branches to show the possibility of a trial, no trial, a hearing coming up, and so on.

For a DUI case, you may have even more variables to diagram. For example, you will want to ask where the potential was pulled over. Were they alone? Where were they headed? Where was the police car? How did they approach? What were the conditions like at the time of the stop? Was it night or day? What was the condition of the side of the road where sobriety tests may have been given? What was the potential wearing?

All these things are really well conveyed visually. Visuals really helps with these kinds of cases. There may not always be a scene, but if there is in any sense of the word, you want to draw a diagram for it.

Again, the branching tree for criminal cases is very important because the timeline going forward is going to be where most of the fear is for the clients. They are going to want to know the possibilities. It is helpful to give someone a sense of where things are going.

For estate planning, that's probably pretty obvious, but it's similar to divorce. You, of course, want to include who has died or who you are doing the planning for. If you're doing a will, you will want to ask the potential who they want their assets to go to. Draw the people involved and the assets out on the diagram. Be sure to include things in the tree such as if there are kids from previous marriage, in-laws, relatives who may cause issues down the line and so on. All this information is critically important.

You should also include branches or possibilities for probate, or a will contest and those types of things. For estate planning, a diagram is critical of the family tree and the family dynamics.

When it comes to real estate law, let's say there is a commercial lease that is at stake or is being disputed. What does the diagram look like? This might be more of just a timeline with payments and perhaps draw out a quick and dirty cash flow calendar if that applies.

Again, I know none of this is alien to you. It's what you do anyway. The difference, however, is up until now you may have only been doing it verbally over the phone or during in person consults. Now you are doing this by video and you really need to engage the potential because of that. Once you start doing it, I think you will love it and like I said, potential clients will love it too. You'll see a dramatic effect.

When it comes to the case outline you can, of course use paper; if you do, I suggest 11x17 so it's big enough to see on camera. As you draw on it, you want to hold it up to the camera and show it as you are making notes. Make sure that you use a black marker and write large enough so that can be seen easily on video. Get familiar doing this so that you know where on the page you have to place certain landmarks, so you don’t run out of room. You don't want to go off the page or have to crunch stuff in the corner. You might even have a quick and easy template you use.

An even better idea than writing this all down on paper, if you can, is to do it on a whiteboard instead. The camera can see the whiteboard very easily. You can stand there with the marker in hand while you talk to the client. They will help you out the information, just as I talked about earlier. You can easily erase it and change the information as needed, or to show other possibilities in the case. Before you erase it, you take a picture of it and send it to the client, or they can take a picture of their screen and save it before moving on. That way you can have as many diagrams as you want. Nothing is lost. Everything is captured on the computer and it can go to the potential client and to you.

Whiteboards are a great involvement device for people to use. Nine times out of ten your clients are going to be calling in from their smartphone or other device and it may not be convenient for them to jot notes down. They're going to be talking and giving you the details. You will do the writing on the board, take a picture and send it to the potential.

Mechanics Of This Involvement Device

Several of our attorney clients agreed to do whiteboard example cases for us. We gave real facts, real scenarios and we didn't have them practice beforehand. The virtual meetings were done live. The results were outstanding. I think once you hear the details of these virtual meetings and my feedback, it will give you a visceral feel for how you can do it. You don't have to do your virtual consults exactly like this, of course. You will make it to fit your style.

Setting The Stage

As you start to do the video consults you will find little changes you will want to make along the way to better your presentation. It might be something as simple as going from headphones with a cord to going wireless. You might notice certain angles where the sunlight comes in or the overhead light makes your coloring off and so on.

I definitely recommend doing a few mock video calls so you can see what your potentials will see.

Get comfortable with your surroundings so everything appears natural.

Remember when are going to talk to the potential, they are preconditioned to work with you if you've used the scripts. You need to maintain that positioning as you continue to talk to the potential. Visual cues are incredibly important to use to your advantage. For example, there are deliberate props you may want to use such as awards or diplomas that may appear behind you on the wall. If you have done a Speak a Book, you might want to set it on your desk facing the camera. There's nothing wrong with these tactics. They are visual cues. You don't have to say anything, but they convey authority. This is very important. You may even want to have a previous case eval on the whiteboard behind you. You could make it a shill type thing and say, "Let me erase this and we can get started. I was just getting done with someone."

A clean whiteboard is a clean start. Even the fact of having the board and you wiping it down indicates to the potential, "Okay. We are ready to begin."

Another visual cue or prop you might consider is having a big stack of files on your desk. You could let the client know, "As you can see, I am pretty busy. These are the whole stack of files that I'm working on. I'm glad you called when you did because I do have time for one or two more cases this month."

All of these visual cues are not meant to be deceptive. They influence how a person thinks and how they're going to perceive you and on average, that's very important. So, you want to appear neat on camera. You don't want to be dressed sloppy or have messy hair, obviously but you don't have to go crazy.

It's not like a job interview where you're perfectly manicured. People understand that you're in a remote environment. Personal items, such as a family picture, are humanizing things. They're actually very good and if you're strategic about it, they can really help you get the prospect and convert them. You would be very surprised. You can even setup deliberate interruptions that serve your purpose.

For example, if you're in an office setting, you may want to have your admin come in and ask you something. You just turn to the admin and say, "I have got about 15 minutes left here. Tell Mr. Smith I'll get right back to him."

Then apologize to your potential for the interruption and go on with the case eval. You can create a little bit of urgency or the appearance of being busy. Again, take this as you will. If you feel it is deceptive, don't do it. However, if it is done the right way it's not going to hurt anybody, and it could help you. On the other hand, you want to keep unplanned interruptions at bay for sure. People coming in and disturbing you is not good unless you're controlling what's happening.

Let your admin and other staff know not to interrupt you. Let the potential client know, "Just so you know, my phone is on silent. I've asked my staff not to come in for the next 30 minutes. I'm all yours."

All these things provide reassuring environmental type cues that will help your conversion.

Now, your environment is set. You know what you're going to show and say. You know how your case eval outline is going to look basically and the steps you'll take to go through it.

When you are transferring into the video call, remember, you have three jobs. One, is to maintain your positioning as an authority. Hopefully, you've used the scripts or had whoever answers the phone use them to position you so you're not going in cold. This will make your job a lot easier. Remember again, maintain your position as an authority.

Like I said, that case eval is incredibly important. You want to get the potential involved. Don't lecture to the person; get them engaged. Have them help you draw the case out. Ask questions. Pause for a second and say, "What do you think about this right here? What should we put here?" and that kind of thing.

You want to demonstrate expertise, but you also want to keep them participating.

You ask, "What's your full name?", and then you write it down.

"What's your wife or husband's name?" and you again, write it down.

"You said you have three kids. OK."

You draw three circles, and so on.

"You were going eastbound. I'm going to draw your car here and the police, how far were they behind you?"

Again, keep the potential involved the whole time in making this picture of their case. Build rapport. Don't interrogate them. Be human. You're on camera so smile a little bit. Show confidence but don't be stone cold. Talk to this person. Ask them how they are doing. Look up at them periodically.

Gain, those are your three jobs; maintain positioning, involve the person and build rapport so that you can ask for the sale.

Putting people at ease is important, especially in the very beginning. You want to give the potential an approximate timeframe of how long you will be talking.

You might say something like, "Just so you know, these consults, usually they go 20 to 30 minutes. We don't usually need to go longer than that. If you need me to go a little faster than that, we might have to reschedule, or we could try to do this quickly in maybe 15 minutes minimum."

Let them know upfront what to expect. Tell the potential what you are going to talk about and that you might have some questions for them along the way. Let them know you are going to be drawing on the whiteboard.

And let them know, "If at any time you can't see me on the camera or important things I'm writing out on the whiteboard, just let me know. I want to make sure that you get something out of this."

Be a human being. Give the potential the lay of the land and get them comfortable. It just makes people feel better.

Then continue to walk them through the rest of the call.

"Like I said, we will do the case eval. I'm going to do all the writing. You're going to listen and give me the details of the case. Then when we are done, I will send you this case eval by email. At the end of the call, I'll ask you what you'd like to do from here."

You're preparing the potential early on that you're going to ask if they want to work with you or not, which is good to do. I would also add at the end of the call, "I'm going to have some homework for you because there are a few additional questions. There are some things I will need to look into a littler deeper and I will need some documents from you after this."

Generally, you aren't going to capture every piece of information you need in that initial call. It's usually not possible.

Tell the potential, "I find that I get the best results when my clients work with me and give me what I need quickly. So, I'll have a little bit of homework. It won't be too onerous, but just to let you know that's what I have for you at the end. I'm going to give you periodic reminders as we go. Remember, our calls are typically 30 minutes. I'm going to tell you when we're at the halfway mark and when we're near the end just so you can keep a sense of time."

Remember your job is to put the person at ease. Tell them what's coming next and you'll have a pretty smooth call.

Early Price Issues & Controlling the Call

(With Script)

The last thing I want to talk about in this section are early price issues and controlling the call. Some of this may be obvious to most of you, while some of it might be a surprise.

If someone asks you about price right up front, it doesn't necessarily mean that they're a bad client. Some people are just prone to bring it up right up front. You may even get that question multiple times throughout the call.

I'm going to provide you with a mini script on how to handle these price questions. Until you have the opportunity to present, do the case eval and really build rapport, answering pricing questions is only going to lead to problems. The potential hasn't experienced you yet. They haven't formed enough of an impression to respect you to move forward. Some people are so cut and dry that it works if price questions are asked and answered up front. However, if someone is not willing to wait 15 or 20 minutes and go through that intake with you, and they are bringing it up multiple times, if you can't defer them, then you've just got to let them go. They just are not in the state of mind where they're going to listen to you right then or they're not controllable. If you can't control a client when you're at the initial consult stage, good luck controlling them once they hire you, if they do. They are going to be a pain and you don't want that.

On the other hand, how do you defer a price? We are going to go over other price issues and how to handle them.

Price deferral script:

Potential Client: "How much do you charge for representation?", or "I already spoke to somebody and they quoted me $1000. How much do you charge?"

These are not the things you want to hear. Some are smoke screens. The potential may be willing to pay you, but they don't trust you yet. They don't know. However, some of these may be valid. The only way to find out, though, is to really challenge them a bit. When they say these things to you, here's what you can say:

You: "Listen, I'm not trying to be slick with you. However, when people ask me how much I charge, I honestly have to tell them it does depend on the complexity of their case. But let me give you a quick example. How much does a car cost? If you want a 600 series Mercedes that performs like a dream, it's going to be $150,000. If you want an old junker that has 100,000 miles, it'll be far cheaper. The same goes with attorneys. So, for me, there are two levels of pricing. You may have a super complex case. Maybe you will need multiple court appearances, expert witnesses, accounting services or other professionals in addition to my legal services. If you absolutely must have a great outcome in your case because your freedom is on the line or maybe you are in the military or have a commercial driver's license, for example, that costs between $15,000 to $30,000.

On the other hand, if your case is simple, or if you only want the bare minimum of legal help, then the cheapest low-level lawyers I know charge $1000 to $1500 for these kinds of cases. Keep in mind though, with everything in life, you get what you pay for.

The good news is that I'm nowhere near the most expensive, but I'm also not the cheapest. So, I've got a quick question for you now. On a scale 1 to 10, 10 being the most expensive, the most work and one being barely any legal work is involved, where do you think your case is going to fall?"

The potential client will give you a number.

You: "OK, great. Well, let's go over your case and then we can see where you're likely going to end up. Even if we don't end up working together, at least you'll have a much clearer idea of what representation may cost you and why."

If you do this right, they will be quiet, and they will go through the rest of the call with you. If you handle this wrong, it's highly likely the potential could just go away or they may just say, "I just can't afford it."

In this case, at least you're giving them a high and a low and you're the potential right off the bat where you fall. They will most likely feel a bit better and you are kind of homing in on a price range without giving them a number. It sort of puts the power back in your hands. If they ask you again about your pricing, as you do the intake, just remind him or her of this.

You: "Listen, on a scale of 1 to 10, you are coming in at about a four. We're getting close to the answer. I need about five to 10 more minutes to get you there. Is that fair?"

If someone gives you a one, you probably don't want to take the case anyway. If someone tells you it's 10, then you may start salivating. Either way you need to ask the potential client that question. Again, it puts the power back in your hands.

Case Evaluations Example & Feedback

Analysis Of A DUI Case Evaluation For Virtual Closing System

Link To Video:

https://www.speakeasymarketinginc.com/case-evaluation-p2/

The first case eval I want to tell you about is one we did with a long time DUI client of ours. To start with, the quality of his video was not fantastic, but it was good enough since he didn't have an HD camera. The attorney was dressed well. He didn't wear a tie or a suit, but he still looked very professional. He looked like an attorney should.

This attorney had a whiteboard ideally positioned right behind him. This showed the potential that he was in an office and he was there to work.

Lawyer: "Do you remember which county you were in when you got arrested?"

Potential Client: "I was in San Francisco. I'm not really sure where that falls."

Attorney: "San Francisco is the city and county of San Francisco, which means your case will take place at 850, Bryant Street, which is the Hall of Justice in San Francisco. One of the nice things about this type of a case in San Francisco, a misdemeanor DUI, which based on some of the information I got from your e-mail, says that you're not going to have to show up in court for some of this case but I can do it for you. So, I can go to the first appearance all the way through the last. For some appearances, it will help that you're there, but I will give you plenty of heads up and make sure you're there with me. But very often I can do the entire case without my client ever having to come to court."

Right off the bat, I can see that this attorney is knowledgeable about DUI cases. He is telling me where my case will be held. He even gives the exact address. Then, early on he tells the potential some good news;

that the person doesn't have to show up to court if she doesn't want to. That should offer the potential some relief. She knows right away that she won't have to sit there in front of a judge and maybe the arresting officer. This client is now going to associate good news and a feeling of comfort with this attorney.

Attorney: "Do you have your paperwork with you?"

Potential Client: "No, not right now."

Attorney: "That's okay. What would really help is once you get your paperwork, if you can just text a picture of the arrest citation you received when you were released from the jail, it will show charges on there. Also, the pink temporary license, which has to do with your driver's license, is good for 30 days. Or we'll get that extended for you since you called me within 10 days of arrest. But I'd like to be able to see that and then assuming you go forward with my services, I can contact the DMV, request a hearing and keep you driving for many months while this case is going on. Hopefully, I can make it so that you never lose your license at all."

What I saw here was that even though the potential client in this case didn't have their paperwork right there, again, the attorney was able to offer immediate and ongoing help and relief. He reassured her that he can help her maintain her driving ability now and into the future. The attorney isn't pushing the potential. He's just giving her the lay of the land. But again, he's offering his help. The potential hasn't hired him yet but is probably starting to feel more comfortable.

Attorney: "Unfortunately, the SFPD vehicles, don't usually have a dash camera, called an MBARS. CHP usually does in California. But what SFPD will have body cameras. So, we should be able to see a lot more of what happened when police came up to the car and then any testing that was done after that."

Again, the attorney here demonstrated specific knowledge of the potential client's case and what was relevant, including certain things that would be helpful to her in the future. In this video he is calm.

He's authoritative. He points to the whiteboard periodically when he needs to make a point. When you use them an involvement device and you engage the potential, they can relax. They see it's a human being. They see that they're not in court, being questioned to death. They're getting information on the screen that they can look at 5, 10, 20, 50 times.

The attorney is cementing his knowledge in this woman's head and is building trust. He's teaching her on the whiteboard. He's empowering her with knowledge, and this comes through from doing this all by video. It would not be nearly as effective by phone.

The attorney uses the whiteboard to put up all sorts of information about the case. He puts it into a format of condensed facts that are all easy to see in one place. There's no sales pitch here. There's only information and a growing feeling of control over the outcome. If I were this potential client, that is how I would feel. I'm getting information, that is easily understood. I'm not looking ahead into the abyss of an unknown nightmare that may be coming. I'm seeing what's probably going to happen. This is very important. The potential has been sitting with the attorney now for 25 minutes; she is engaged.

This attorney is offering the potential a tailored outcome or a tailored set of possibilities.

Attorney: "Of course you can handle your DUI case by yourself if you want. However, you're going to wonder for the rest of your life, what would have happened if you had hired a lawyer. How would that have changed things? The first thing that I am going to try and do for you, is win the case. If we win the case, all that goes away. Nothing happens, you get to drive. You don't have to get extra insurance. You don't have to do a DUI school. You are not on probation. You don't have a criminal conviction on your record. There's no jail or work program. It's huge for employment purposes because if you win, there's no conviction on your record. That's the goal.

If we can't flat out win the case then the next thing, we're trying to do is negotiate for a reduction of charges. A reduction of charges would mean less penalty. If we can't do that, we might go to jury trial where it would take 12 people in a box to all say guilty for you to be convicted. It could potentially be worse but in a lot of counties they don't penalize you that much worse. It's just a lot more expensive and a lot more stress. So here we could win by getting them dismiss the charges or going to jury trial. This is why when I had the other chart up, showing just different months...."

The attorney was giving the potential various future scenarios and giving the likelihood of each. He told the potential the upside and the downside of each. The potential now has a very clear picture of what may happen, depending on which of the branches or forks in the road she chooses to go down. They don't have to mentally keep all this in their head. On the phone, frightened out of her mind and not thinking or hearing clearly, the potential is unlikely to retain much information. Over a typical 30 to 40-minute call, 90% of the information the attorney gave her would have been lost. With a video, recall can be 50% or higher.

Additionally, screenshots of all of the information the attorney went over will be sent to the client as well. All of this offers you a competitive advantage over the guys who are still only doing phone consults.

Analysis Of A Divorce Case Evaluation For Virtual Closing System

Link To Video:

https://www.speakeasymarketinginc.com/case-evaluation-p4/

I did a critique of a case evaluation for a family law attorney that I am going to tell you about. Unfortunately, it wasn't the best I have seen, but it also wasn't the worse. Regardless, there are important things that you will be able to take away from the feedback I provided this attorney.

Attorney: "I saw from the intake paperwork that you turned in that you have two kids. Do you happen to have any pictures handy on your phone? Yeah, I'd like to see the kids here. "

Potential Client: "I'll send you some. I've got two beautiful little girls."

Attorney: "That's wonderful. Just so you know, we're a kid friendly and kid-centric kind of firm. Kids come first and it's something that we like you to know right from the beginning. It's not really appropriate for us to necessarily meet them and interact with them a lot but it's good for us to get a feel for them."

First things first, initially, she shows great empathy. We want that. However, right off the bat, she's assuming that children are the most important facets of the whole divorce. While that might be true in most cases, that is not necessarily the case for everyone. For some people, other facets are more important. Additionally, one thing to note is that she asked for photos of the kids. It shows that she assumes the potential will be hiring her. That could be off putting to some people. That may ruin the consultation right then and there. That's overreaching. Its overstepping. The attorney doesn't know yet whether this potential is comfortable with that or not. Again, to assume that kids are the number one issue, it's probably a safe assumption, but not necessarily the right one.

It's always better to ask, "What is the most important aspect of this case for you?"

That's a far better question, because then the potential gives you the answer and you know where he or she stands.

Attorney: "Is there a relationship with your husband at this time, in terms of the cordiality or lack thereof of your interactions? Do you feel safe? Are you economically stable? Are there any of those types of concerns? Or are you concerned for the welfare of your children at all when they're around him?"

Potential Client: "We're still living together but he will be, I think, surprised if and when I file. My biggest concern right now is how do I keep the children for the majority of the time, while we go through this. He's just an angry person. He's not violent or anything like that but really not a pleasure to be around right now. And I imagine after this, it's going to be, of course even worse."

The attorney actually did something positive here by bringing up several different scenarios that could be of issue for the potential. However, on the other hand she may be asking too many questions up front. It would have been better to structure the questions instead of just firing off, "What about this? What about that?" and so on.

The potential might not remember everything being asked if he or she is under stress. It's better to slowly step them through it. Instead the attorney could have broken it down.

"Is economic security one of your biggest concerns? What about custody and visitation rights?"

Allow the potential to answer and then continue with, "Are you worried about your safety at all? Is there any domestic violence or other potential issues I should know about?"

It's better to walk people through all of this one step at a time versus just hammering away with questions all at once. Again, the potential client is describing her situation, but she needs more guidance.

Attorney: "OK. Well, I'm relieved to hear that you're not anticipating any violence and that there hasn't been any previously. I will say if things start to swing that way and you start to think it might occur, I would encourage you to reach out to me right away. We can conduct a lot of this in stealth mode, so to speak, until we're ready to pull the trigger and have him served if that's a concern. Things can go from zero to domestic violence very quickly, unfortunately and your safety and that of your children is paramount."

Here the attorney did a great job offering comfort to the potential client and ways to work on the case in the event the husband starts getting physically abusive, yelling and screaming, hitting her, and so on. That's really positive. It was also really smart of the attorney to mention that there are ways to work on the case without the potential involvement of the husband or the husband knowing, which is excellent. That's good.

There were a few things to point out in this particular case eval that this attorney could work on. First, her lighting was very poor, and the camera angle was not optimal. She had the camera positioned on the table well below her so, to the potential she is literally being talked down to just a bit, which is not good for the power dynamic. Ideally, the attorney should position the camera across the table, straight up and down. Also, for this attorney, unfortunately the glare on the whiteboard made it hard to see what she was writing down. This is another reason it is important to do a few test runs and record yourself so you can see what the potential will see.

Also, this attorney, frankly, just dressed too casually for the seriousness of this issue in this case. She was wearing a polo and jeans. I recommend wearing something comfortable and natural looking, but also it needs to be professional.

Additionally, the quality of the video in this case evaluation was not great. You can buy a great HD camera for a reasonable price, which I highly recommend. This is all online and things go wrong but why not make that small investment and just make sure at least you can control the quality of the video.

Back to this case eval, the attorney did end up asking the potential client to do several homework assignments, which helped with engagement. You don't want to give huge lists of things you want the potential to do, but just a few shows you are invested. I know having dealt with several legal situations myself, you're emotional. You're scared and you're overwhelmed. As the attorney, you have to do everything possible to reduce those anxieties for the potential.

Attorney: "There's going to be a significant amount of financial disclosure and review. We're going to ask you for information on everything. It can get very expensive to investigate financials when you aren't aware of what you have or what your name is on. So as much guidance as you can give us, to focus our discovery in terms of financial disclosures, that would be very helpful. If your husband forthcoming, then it will go smoothly, and it won't be a problem. You don't have to have access to the accounts necessarily. But if you have noted any statements come in, with names of creditors or other bills, put that on your list."

In this interaction, the attorney was offering helpful advice on how the potential can help with their own case. Again, the homework. It's not overwhelming, and she asked for it in a real organic way. I liked how she explained everything, and it wasn't done as a demand.

She also mentioned, again, issues that were tailored to talking to a woman. If you think this is sexist, I'm sorry, but it's just the case. I've seen this attorney walk us through how she talks to a male client, the way she does it is quite different. The good thing is that both ways that she talks are very tailored to the gender of the person.

What I noticed here, was the way she was speaking to the potential. In my experience, is more of how women deal with issues. Again, I'm a man and I deal with things differently. For example, the way the attorney talked about potential domestic violence, unfortunately, more often that is a concern for women and children. Again, stereotypical all the way, whatever you want to call. However, it's just a fact. Again, she tailored the questions and conversation to speak to a woman. When I saw this attorney do a case eval with a male, she changed what and how she spoke. You want to do that with all of your potential clients, obviously. You may tailor your presentation to relate to your audience.

Lastly for this attorney's critique I want to address the whiteboard and diagraming she did. She ended up only writing out the timeline going forward, which the potential had actually asked for several different timelines several times. The initial whiteboard she drew up was good. The engagement was good, but engagement needed to be maintained throughout the whole presentation.

For example, she drew up the one diagram or timeline on the whiteboard and talked for 20 minutes. There wasn't much engagement. My recommendation instead, is to draw up a past fact pattern and background, then the diagram of the scene or the family tree, then another diagram of what may happen in the future; a branching tree diagram. This could include things like how long the case could take, what potential things could change in the case and so on. All three diagrams really are the minimum you should have in your white boarding process to keep total engagement.

Analysis Of A Domestic Violence Case Evaluation For Virtual Closing System

Link To Video:

https://www.speakeasymarketinginc.com/case-evaluation-p5/

The next analysis I want to tell you about what for a domestic violence case for the Virtual Closing System.

Attorney: "I'm going to just ask you some questions. I know this has been an extremely emotional time for you and the rest of the family. You can cut me off at any point in time if there's something that you don't want to forget or whatnot. I did get some information from you through the website and I appreciate you taking the time to fill that out. It gives me a little bit of an idea of what we're dealing with. I kind of have a good handle on how we're going to properly defend you, strategize for things down the road and whatnot because with these domestic violence cases, emotions are always running high. I understand you also have children so that can be really difficult."

This attorney shows empathy immediately, which is great. That's really important, especially in these types of cases.

Attorney: "A little quick background on me. I used to be a prosecutor in LA County. I worked within the family violence unit for a brief period of time. I've handled hundreds, if not thousands of these cases from the start of when I was a prosecutor 20 years ago and I've had my own defense practice now for 17 plus years."

The attorney gives his background and he is specifically able to match the potential client's situation to his experience. Why? Because he tells her I've worked as a former prosecutor in the family violence unit in Los Angeles. He's seen hundreds to thousands of these kinds of cases. He's demonstrating very specifically that he has the background, he has the knowledge. He tells her he knows a lot about these cases and that, in a way, he's seen it all. This is a great demonstration within the first minute and a half of specifics he can relate to in the potential's case.

Attorney: "I understand the process of how prosecutors look at these cases and, how they analyze them when they're determining what to file, whether to file and how the case moves through the system, not just in court, but also prior to getting the courts."

Here he demonstrates that he understands, and he knows these cases from the prosecutor's perspective; what the prosecutor thinks, when they're going to file, how they're going to file, how aggressive they're going to be. Again, he is demonstrating on multiple fronts that he knows these cases and he knows them from the perspective that's important to the client, the prosecutor. The attorney has showed here that he has specific knowledge, and he's pacing through the whole thing too, in the order that he presents it.

Attorney: "I need you to be totally honest with me about everything. I've heard it all, so don't be embarrassed. This way, I know how best to handle and protect you through this process, not only on the legal side, but also on the emotional and personal side. I know we don't really know each other that well, but I'm married myself. I have children. I know what kind of stresses this can present. I've heard it all. Just be honest with me so I know how to best strategize and protect you throughout this whole process."

It's great that the attorney is telling the client to be honest with him and tell him everything. He is telling him he has heard it all before and there is no reason to be embarrassed. Why? He is reassuring the potential and making him feel comfortable. He also shares his own person information which makes him more relatable. He's telling her on multiple levels that he understands and the reasons why. This particular attorney is great at demonstrating empathy and matching himself to that potential client.

The next step he took with the client was to do the whiteboarding. This attorney was very well dressed or camera ready. He looks professional. He has nice clothing. He's not too formal, but he looks good. He also positioned himself to take the video call in a quiet place. There are no distractions, which is very important.

As with any case evaluation we noticed a few things he could have done better. For example, this attorney didn't use an HD camera, so the image wasn't crystal clear. Again, don't go crazy and spend thousands of dollars on a web cam. You can get something basic and at a reasonable price but just make sure it is HD. If you do the basics, it makes you look better. It ups your game.

The whiteboarding he did looks clear and the text was readable. However, if he had an HD camera, it would have been much easier for the potential to see the writing on the board. Again, the more professional you look, the clearer you look, the more people can see expressions on your face and get a real feel for you as a person. Remember, communication is not just what you hear, but also the body language of the attorney. The better you look, the higher value your perceived services will appear. You will look more capable.

Additionally, if you use an HD camera you can always record your own videos and put them on your website to use for marketing as well. If you want to improve even further, there's a lighting kit you can purchase for about $150.

This attorney was in a plain, white room, which is fine. The attention should be on what he was saying and writing and not necessarily on the background. He could have added some awards or pictures in the background to make him more human but that isn't always necessary. He also could have used other props, maybe an example of a court summons and walk the prospect through what it looks like. The other thing this attorney might need to watch is that he used a lot of abbreviations to keep his writing shorthand. Now, you don't want to write every single word out or it will get too crowded. However, you don't want the potential to come back and look at the pictures of the board later and not remember what anything stood for or what it meant.

You also want to make sure of little things like the color of marker you use on the whiteboard. This attorney used lighter colors. I would stick with blacks and reds.

For the timeline, this attorney wrote everything vertical. I would make sure and write everything out landscape. That way you can maybe write two or three timelines and it is easier to read this way.

A Critique Of Auto Accident Case Evaluation

Link To Video:

https://www.speakeasymarketinginc.com/case-evaluation-p6/

Potential Client: "I was in an accident last Friday. It was a rear end collision, and I am experiencing some pain. I just don't know if I have a claim or not."

Attorney: "OK. Can you tell me how it happened?"

Potential Client: "I was on the 101 Freeway and I was rear ended by a gentleman. I don't know if he just wasn't paying attention, but I slowed down and was hit from behind."

Attorney: "How bad was the impact?"

Potential Client: "It was pretty bad. I mean, my car is totaled and I'm in some pretty bad pain."

Attorney: "Have you seen a doctor so far?"

Potential Client: "I have."

Attorney: "Have you been contacted by either the other driver or his insurance company?"

Potential Client: "I didn't know if I was supposed to do it or not."

Attorney: "OK. Have you ever been through anything like this before?"

Potential Client: "I haven't. No."

Attorney: "There's a first time for everything, unfortunately. So, what questions do you have for me?"

For this case evaluation the attorney set up his whiteboard in a place that looked like a temporary spot. The good thing is that it is set up against a ton of lawbooks, which traditionally is a good thing. But again, the whiteboard seems to be attached on an impromptu basis or a temporary basis. Why not hang some plaques and awards up there and a law license or two? That would be good and would help with the credibility.

The attorney for this case eval was, again, well dressed. He was very friendly with the potential, but he waited too long to start diagramming. At the very least it would have been good for him to lay out the scene of the accident right away. He also asked what questions she has of him. But before he asked this, it would have been better if he established his authority and credentials first instead asking right away what questions the potential had for him.

Attorney: "Well, I've been doing this for 42 years. All 42 years has been plaintiff personal injury cases, and that includes handling motor vehicle collisions, slip and falls, medical malpractice and all sorts of bodily injury cases. I do not represent insurance companies. So, this is exactly what I do, and I have been doing for my entire legal career."

Here he starts explaining his background and that he has 42 years of experience, which is a lot, but he says he represents plaintiffs. It would be better to say that he represents people who have been in auto accidents. Speak in simple terms that a potential can understand. Otherwise, he could have explained to the potential client that he would become a plaintiff if he files the case. For someone who is not an attorney, the legalese language can be confusing. A client is not going always going to know who a plaintiff is and who is a defendant or what that means. They may be in pain from the accident. They may be frightened to talk to an attorney at all. A lot of people are, so you should be especially careful not to overwhelm them from the start with the legalese of the case.

In the intro, this attorney also mentions that he does handle slip and falls and medical malpractice. He already knows that this potential client is talking about auto accidents, so that's really not relevant. There's no need to bring that up now.

Potential Client: "Will I get to work with you or are there other attorneys I will work with?"

Attorney: "I'm a sole practitioner. I run my own shop, so you will always deal with me. You will also deal with my secretary, Barbara. She's been with me for 27 years and there is also my paralegal, Roxanne. She's been with me for 30 years. Everybody here works to serve our clients, although everybody has their own area of expertise. I'm a lawyer. My paralegal works very closely with my clients, collecting medical records and getting the documentation. My legal secretary handles the pleadings and the lawsuits and other necessary court issues."

Here, the potential client asked if she'd be working with him or other attorneys and he details for her that he is the only attorney, but also gives specific information about his secretary and legal secretary and the length of time they have been with him. This shows he is very stable. He's been in this game a long time. That is very comforting for a potential. He also explains his staff's roles, which helps as well. This way the potential knows who she will be communicating with when contacting the office.

Attorney: "Do you know what the value of what car would be if you had decided to sell it to someone the day before the collision?"

Potential Client: "I think probably around 15."

Attorney: "Okay, what you may want to do is look at kelleybluebook.com and it will give you a sense of what the range of values might be given the car's make, model, mileage, condition and equipment. You should have that in mind because at some point we're going to get offers from the other party's insurance company. They're going to have to pay the fair market value of the car and it's a good idea to have a bit of a heads up to know whether they're low balling you or not. If you haven't been contacted by the other party's insurance company yet, there may be some delay. It might be that the at fault guy hasn't even reported it to his carrier yet. That's where your auto insurance again comes in. Did you carry collision coverage on your car?"

Potential Client: "Yes."

Attorney: "Do you know what your deductible is?"

Potential Client: "$500, I think."

Attorney: "Okay. You've got a $500 deductible, and what that means is typically you can go to your insurance company and they will take care of the total loss subject to the first $500; which they will not pay, you have to pay. In cases where it's clear liability, I would say it's more than 50% of the time, your insurance company will waive your deductible here. They know they're going to get it from the other insurance company. Instead of waiting for the other insurance company to get involved, you can go ahead and go to your insurance company and start this process."

Although dealing with the car damage isn't usually part of a personal injury case this attorney handles, he is taking the time to go through these steps with her. He asks her about her insurance and then tells her how it works and how and why she can take care of some aspects of her case right away. This is a really good thing to do. Some attorneys would simply tell a potential that they don't deal with anything that has to do with repairs or replacement of the vehicle. They might just tell the potential to call their insurance and that's it.

For the visual aspect of this attorney's case eval, he used the whiteboard. However, he could have added more details such as his categories could have used some titles on them.

He did do a timeline which was good. However, I would have liked for the attorney to actually diagram out the scene of the accident. He could have added details like the direction the cars were moving in, type of road, the weather conditions, the speed, and so on. That all can be encapsulated in the diagram with some words and arrows drawn in.

In an auto accident case, the diagram is very important.

CHAPTER 9

MODULE #3: PRESENT

In Module 3, we will talk about asking for the sale. This is where a lot of attorneys drop the ball.

First, before you get to asking for the sale, you should make sure you have answered all the potential's questions. You don't want to move ahead and then all of the sudden the sale falls apart because you didn't spend enough time in the previous modules being thorough with the case eval.

Before you get to this step, you want to be sure you have given the potential the full lay of the land. You want to reiterate, "Well, listen, we've gone over your case. We've done this case eval, which I'm going to send to you. I want to ask you a couple of questions here, because we're coming to the end."

You want to give the potential a timeline. For example, for a personal injury client, you could say, "I've handled a lot of cases like yours. You're looking at four to five months from here until the case is resolved. If the insurance company plays ball, we're looking at probably 90 days until you have the check in hand. If the insurance company doesn't play ball, this can go on for up to a year. I have the feeling based on this company that they're going to play ball. We're not asking for a crazy amount. We are just asking for what is fair."

Let's say its divorce. Same thing. You say something like, "This whole process is probably going to take about six to seven months to get that final decree."

Nobody wants to sit with an open legal situation. Give the potential a timeline of the major events that are coming and when.

Another example would be for estate planning, you could say, "We're going to set up this trust and it's going to take about 10 days to get everything in place."

For when the potential has been arrested, the conversation might start, "Now there's going to be a series of hearings so we're looking at this whole case taking probably a year."

Then you can continue on with letting them know all of the different hearings that will occur and when.

When you are getting near the end of the conversation, you might set up the next step by saying, "O.k. we have gone over a lot here. That being said, I don't have all of the information I will need to run with your case. There's going to be some homework on your end. If you want the best representation, I need you to help me out a little bit. So, here's where I'm going to need from you ...".

Then you let the potential know what further information you will need and when or what paperwork you need back and why and again when. Then don't forget to restate what they earlier told you was the thing they are most concerned about.

"Just so you know, I know that you told me that resolving X, Y or Z is the most important thing to you in this legal situation, so I'm going to keep this top of mind the whole time that we work together on your case. I want to let you know. That's why I asked you the question; because I'm going to hold that up in front of me and make all decisions with you, with your approval considering that goal. I just want you to know that," you could say.

All of these things we have just covered are important in order to lay the groundwork to then ask for the sale. If you don't do these things, you're much more likely to receive excuses and objections.

If you can get things down to where most of your initial consults either consummate and have no objections or they blow up right at the beginning, that's good; that means you're doing the right thing. The tire kickers, you're kicking them out and the people that really have a case, you're getting them, unless something crazy happens. You will get them if you prepare the groundwork properly.

Now, asking for the sale is the hardest, scariest and sometimes most disappointing moment in this initial consult. Remember, you paid for the marketing. The phone rang. You got them on to video conference with you. You went through all of your scripts and heard the information about their case. You did the eval and spent time and money.

The last thing you want to hear is any ridiculous excuse from the potential and then they disappear into thin air. I understand this but you can't let that choke you or make you afraid to ask for the sale. We are setting up a process here where you should be confident in what you're doing, as long as you practice the things we have talked about.

What you could say here, in summary, is, "Listen, based on the facts of your case so far, I think there's a really good likelihood that we're going to meet the most important goal of yours or at least come very close."

If you want to try a more direct approach you could say, "Is there anything we haven't covered or any reason you're not ready to get started working together?"

Within the *Virtual Closing System* there are scripts that accompanies this so you could also use that script.

Whatever you do say, pause and then let the potential talk. Pause and hear what they have to say. If they say they are ready to move on, then move to module four, where you reveal three-tier price and close.

Often the potential will come up with some sort of excuse such as, "Let me think about it. I want to talk to my husband," or "I can't afford it right now", or "I want to talk to other attorneys".

You need to probe the potential gently and in the right way to find out if their excuse is real or a smoke screen. Often, it's just a smokescreen. You haven't really gotten to the bottom of the real reason why they're saying no. But if it's the real reason, you'll find that out, too. Again, using the scripts, you can find out.

You could say something like, "Mr. Smith, by X date, you really need to decide what you want to do in your case and based on my experience, these are the options."

Refer to the timeline and show the potential what happens if he or she does nothing versus if they act.

"You can sit there and do nothing or speak to whoever you need, think about it and then make a decision. But I recommend you do it by this date. Here are some appointment times for us to follow up or you if you are ready to move forward let's get started so you can start to feel some relief right away."

Lay of the consequences of waiting out for the potential to see. For a DUI potential you could remind him or her of what is going to happen to their driver's license if they act now versus waiting. You might ask, "Do you need to drive a lot? How are you going to get the kids to school? How are you going to get to work?"

Regardless of the time of case, you want to mention both the actual consequences and the emotional ones to prompt the potential to move forward. I call it "future pacing"; not taking action versus taking action now.

For estate planning matters, you might say, "If you wait to start your estate planning and something happens unexpectedly before you get to it, there are a number of negative things that could happen. If someone dies without a will, for example, called dying intestate. That means probate and that means a lot of money, a lot of time and probably not much left over for you. You don't want that to happen. So, take action now or there may be some major issues down the road if something happens."

For criminal defense, the potential may have an arraignment coming up or perhaps for a DUI the deadline for filing action to keep their driver's license is looming. All of these things are levers you can push to get the client to move.

For an auto accident case, you can warn the potential that the longer they wait to move on hiring an attorney, the longer it is going to take to get a settlement. That could be a huge in a personal injury case. The injuries suffered may have put the potential out of work. You want to remind the person why they shouldn't wait.

With a divorce case, there could be an imminent threat that the other party may file first. There could be issues with custody that are time sensitive. In these cases, specifically there will certainly be an emotional toll and people tend to want to put off having to deal with those types of things. However, it's good to remind the potential that the sooner he or she moves, the sooner they can move on.

For a business law case, it could be a situation where the potential has a commercial lease that's coming up for renewal in a month. If the person waits, that leaves less time for negotiating or for finding a new space, for example.

What I'm trying to communicate here with these examples, is that it doesn't matter the practice area. There are always reasons to act now versus later. You are the attorney, so you know these things better than I do. But the point is, you should have those reasons ready before you speak to the potential. Then you don't have to scramble when you hear their excuses to delay.

~~~~~~~~~~~~~~~~~~~~~~~~~~~~~~

Excuses And Objections When You Ask For The Sale

This is the script that will help you when the potential gives excuses and objections when you ask for the sale. No one likes this part but it's especially important to address and this script will help you quite a bit.
~~~~~~~~~~~~~~~~~~~~~~~~~~~~~~

Here we will use a DUI case as an example.

Attorney: "Based on the facts and circumstances of your case as I understand them, I'm confident that I can help you, especially with your most important question, (here's where you state their most important question or most important need). You told me it's critical that you keep your driver's license because you're a long-distance trucker. So, I know because of your impending DUI situation, the most important thing is to keep that license, if possible. I'm confident that I can help you, especially in that area. I can't guarantee a good outcome and frankly, I'm not even allowed by my state bar to do so. But I am confident I can have a real positive impact on your case. With that being said, is there anything we haven't covered that would prevent you from getting started with me as your attorney today?"

Now, that question is hard to ask. It takes balls to ask that question. No one is good at it without a lot of practice. When asking for the sale, you should always give a reason why by restating their most important need. This way, the potential knows they are being listened to. A lot of attorneys don't do this. They just kind of go on with their pitch, without giving a reason why it is imperative the potential acts now. Either the client will agree to move forward or will give a reason or reasons not to.

Potential Client: "No, there's no reason. That sounds good. Let's go ahead."

If the potential wants to go ahead and hire you, that's great. Move on to module four in this book where you will review your retainer agreement and collect payment. If, on the other hand, the potential throws up an objection or an excuse as to why they can't or don't want to move forward just yet, continue on below.

Potential Client: "I have to think about it."

Potential Client: "I have to talk to my husband or wife."

Potential Client: "I want to go talk to other attorneys first."

Attorney: "Listen, I respect your choice and your decision, but I'm obligated to tell you just a few things. Based on my 17 years of experience and having handled over 200 cases in this area, I'm going to give you an idea of your options from here.

You can:

1. Do nothing and just wait.

2. You can speak to whoever you need speak to, which is fine, including other attorneys if you want.

3. You can retain me as your attorney today and we move this ball forward right now.

I want to go over these options and it's important that you understand this.

Option one, do nothing and wait so you don't have to take action today. If you do nothing, here's what's likely to happen in the next X number of days, weeks or months ..."

Here you will explain to the potential the negative effects of not hiring an attorney right now and how that will hurt their case.

Attorney: "If you're going to wait, please, whatever you do and whoever you hire, I wouldn't wait for longer than X days (and keep this short, don't say weeks or months) to prevent those things I told you about earlier from happening.

The second option is you wait and speak to whoever you need to speak to. But schedule a follow up call with me in the next 3 to 7 days, max. You could always cancel it if you need to, if you change your mind you decide to go with someone else. But I've seen a lot of folks just sit on a decision until it's too late and their backs are against the wall. I don't want to see that happen to you. As of now anyway, I do have a few openings in my calendar if you want to go ahead and set up a follow up call. I have tomorrow at 6:00. I have Tuesday at 4:00 and I have Wednesday at 3:00. Which one will work best for you?"

Offer them a few dates and times. But again, always include the reason why.

Attorney: "You third option would be to retain me as your attorney today and we can move this thing forward. If you take action today in probably 20 minutes or so, you're going to feel a whole heck of a lot better. A lot of my clients do because you know you took action. You're working on your situation. It's going to get better from here. So, those are the three options. What do you think is the best thing for you to do from here?"

Pause and wait for the answer. You have spelled it out for the potential and you're not showing neediness and you're showing you are okay with whatever they do. That's why this script is really powerful. Pretty much no one can get mad at you if you do this, because, again, you're giving a reason why. You've given them whatever they want to do and there's no pressure. It's logical. You're going to get a much better response at this point. They may say they are just going to wait. That's okay. They may try to schedule the follow up call. That's no problem. Get them scheduled. If they want to speak to someone else, like I said, you can let them know that's okay too.

In some cases, they may say, "Well, listen, I can't schedule right now. I just have to think about it."

If you hear something like this, it means that you haven't gotten to the real reason that they don't want to schedule a second appointment with you. If you've gotten this far and you've used these scripts, you shouldn't hear that. However, if you do, that means there is some reason you haven't uncovered that is causing this person to hesitate. They will probably go away and never come back.

If you get to that point you could say, "Listen, it sounds like this is not for you. I won't try to keep you but if you wouldn't mind, for my future potential clients, what was it? What did I miss? I want to improve my game."

Sometimes they may tell you, while other times they may continue to avoid saying the real reason.

Either way, this is the best way to handle these objections. It's far better than what I see most attorneys do now which is simply letting it go.

It's going to take some time and practice to do this with confidence. However, once you do master these techniques, it's going to help you quite a bit. I think you will be surprised at the efficacy of it and how much more business you are going to get.

CHPATER 10

MODULE #4: THE CLOSE

In module four we are going to talk about reviewing your retainer agreement, getting the signature and collecting payment.

You are probably in the home stretch at this point, but it's not over until the money is in the bank or the check clears. You'd be surprised at the last minute how things can arise to kill your deal. Don't let off the gas.

In this module we go over all of these things to consider ensuring you make it to home plate.

Next, we will talk about negotiating your fees. A three-tier price structure works far better than just saying, "This is my price. Take it or leave it."

When you do give your three-tier price, this leaves you some wiggle room. You want to be able to say, "Listen, I know you're having a hard time with this. If you can make the decision today and we can get started now, I'll take off an extra $200."

Leave yourself that room as a last resort when all else fails. You are probably thinking, "Why do I want to do that?"

At this point you have presented a price. Perhaps you had to negotiate a bit. The next step is to go through your retainer agreement. Remember, even when you get the agreement initialed and signed, that's only partial insurance that this is a done deal. It's not full because you haven't gotten paid yet. They can still run away at this point.

There are a few ways I want to suggest to you about retainers to make them more likely to be signed. First, you want it in plain English, not legalese. No one likes it. If the potential can't understand what's in the contract, this could cause them to put up walls and not want to sign. You don't want that. You want them to feel like it makes sense. Even the font size, font type spacing, and length are all important factors. Keep it simple with black print on white paper so it's easy to see.

I recommend thirteen-point font or bigger so everyone can easily read it. It's less intimidating. When it comes to the length of the agreement, keep it concise if you can. You won't be able to cover every contingency. It's not possible and if you try to make an agreement that covers every contingency, that means something's wrong with your process and something's wrong with your client selection. There's no agreement on earth that will hold everybody in. There just isn't. There will always be a small percentage of the population, that will try to find a loophole, will give you trouble by not paying, whatever it is. However, 90% to

95% of the population will do what's asked of them in the agreement because they're afraid of being sued. They're afraid of the unethical part of reneging on an agreement, that kind of thing. Again, keep it short and make it in plain English so anyone can understand what is in the document and I suggest double spacing, so everything is easy to read.

When it comes to reviewing the actual document and signing, you will want to use an e-signature service. We recommend DocuSign. We use this service for all our agreements because it's easy. It's simple. You can even customize various fields within eDocuSign.

eDocuSign is relatively inexpensive. If you're sending and getting back, 5, 10, 15 contracts a month for a retainer, you're not going to care.

When preparing the information, you need to prepare the agreement beforehand. Make sure everything is formatted correctly and there should be several points within the contract where the potential needs to initial. Really this doesn't make the agreement any stronger. However, it gives the potential smaller commitments along the way, before they get to the final signature.

When you set up the agreement with initial requirements along the way, it always helps facilitate a sale versus just a long document and then a final signature at the end. If you do little initials along the way, it's like walking the potential along with baby steps. They are just agreeing to one paragraph at a time and then one more, and so on and so forth.

The payment information should be included within the agreement itself. Don't do it separately. It should include what form of payments you accept, along with a place to add the actual payment information, billing address and so on.

This will help you too in case there are chargebacks or other disputes. Now, not only has the potential agreed to your representation, they have also put their payment information in there, too. It makes it a lot stronger.

Now when it comes to the point of reviewing the agreement, you will want to go through it with the potential. Don't just give them the agreement, tell them to read it and get it back to you. That's dropping the ball, big time. You want to tell them, "We're going to go through the retainer agreement together. I'm going to explain each paragraph as we go so you understand and make sure you don't have any lingering questions. So, let's do that now."

Hold their hand until the very end. Explain what is in each part and have them initial as they go through it with you. Small commitments; small steps. Psychologically, this moves the person along and makes them feel comfortable. When you get to the final signature at the end of the document, make sure everything is complete and then move on to collecting payment.

There is always the question from attorneys on who should be doing the actual collecting of payments. Some people will say, "Okay, great. Thanks for getting that signed. Now I'm going to have Susan collect your payment."

This is actually a very bad idea. You want to collect the payment right then and there if you can. There are two schools of thought here. Some of the professionals we work with don't want to deal at all with payment. They have their admin, or a secretary do it. The truth is, however, whoever is collecting the payment has to care about getting that money as much as you do and that can be rare. It doesn't matter who they are, even if they have scripts. So, as uncomfortable as it may be, initially you want to do this so that you can control the whole process. There's no chance to drop the person. There's no chance for a different personality to disrupt the rapport you have built.

When it comes to what forms of payment to accept, you should try to stay away from checks or cash payments. If someone must stop to make out a check to you, that breaks up the flow of the appointment. Same thing if they plan on paying in cash in person. This interrupts the flow you may never hear from him again, even if they have signed a retainer.

Keep the payment to online forms only, whether it's PayPal, credit card or whatever it might be. Of course, there will be small fees for online payments, and you may want to pad your fee to absorb those small costs. However, you can also use this to make the client feel better. You could say, "I take payment through PayPal and by credit card. I'm going to pay the fees for it. Don't worry. Just send me the amount due and whatever fees they charge; I will pay for it."

It's a nice concession for the potential and it's a much classier, less friction filled way to handle it.

Make sure you can accept most of the major credit cards, PayPal and Venmo. The more ways you can accept payment, the better. If you only accept a limited number of payment methods, some people may say, "Oh, I don't have this, but I have that."

If you don't accept that form of payment, you may lose the sale right there. So, don't limit yourself to one way. It's also important to be familiar with using all the different payment systems. Also, it seems simple, but know your own usernames and logins so you don't have to scramble. If you have to go look for anything, this causes friction and breaks the momentum. You don't want any friction. Now is the time to get that money before anything can cause a disruption.

You also need to test these systems on your own before you get to the point of accepting payment from the client. Some of these system like Venmo and PayPal, require you to do several test payments. You may want to send a dollar to the client, for example, just to make sure the banking information is correct on both sides and everything works well. Then have the client send you the test payment back, again just to make sure everything is smooth when you get to the actual retainer fee payment. I know it sounds crazy, but it activates what's called the "law of reciprocity" and it helps facilitate payment.

Again, you want every little edge you can get, to get that payment successfully from the client. Then while you're working on verifying the payment, you want to give yourself an excuse to do something. Let's say again, you do Venmo or credit card, whatever it is, once you get their information, now you call in your assistant.

"Hey, Mike. Can you run this? Here it is. I'm in the middle of talking with Mrs. Smith here, so I would appreciate if you can handle this so I can continue speaking with her."

Then, get back on the call or the video chat and let the client know, "I'm having Mike run the payment. While I'm doing that, let me get that case eval over to you. I'm also going to send you a copy of my book and I will also get you a copy of the agreement. I'm sending all of that now, to your email."

Keep the person engaged even while the payment is being processed. Again, all of this should be practiced with your staff or by yourself, if you are the one running the entire show.

Once you have the signed agreement and the payment, the fun starts. You get to go to work. At this point, you want to pay attention to have a really robust new client onboarding process.

This will reduce buyer's remorse, which a lot of people have. They feel bad. They realize they have just parted with thousands of dollars. You want to make sure that you continue to reassure the client that they did the right thing. This part is critical. You also need to give them an idea of what to expect next.

"Okay, great. We have the agreement and your payment. We're all set. I'm going to get working on your case. I'm going to e-mail you tonight and, in the next 3 days, please get that homework into me; those documents I need. I'm going to have my office follow up with you on Thursday. We have your first court hearing next week (or whatever might be coming up, depending on the client's circumstances)."

You need to give the client expectations and again, reiterate what's going to happen. As the case goes on, you want to keep doing that. You will need a continual follow-up system for that. This is outside of the scope our *Virtual Closing System*. However, that is something you can still contact us about. This step is very important. If you do this and you do it right, your payments will continue to go through uninterrupted because the client feels secure that you are actually doing the work for them. You will get positive reviews instead of no reviews or bad reviews.

I know you might be thinking at this point that you have already done all this work to retain the client and to get the payment, shouldn't that be enough? Sorry, the answer is no. However, the updates and continued follow-up throughout the case doesn't necessarily have to be you. This is something your staff definitely can be trained on.

Each case must be managed cradle to grave.

Presenting Your Three-Tier Pricing And Negotiation, If The Potential Client Doesn't Like Your Pricing

In Module 4, this script will cover what to do if the potential client doesn't like your pricing.

Attorney: "OK. All right. Let's review my fees for taking on your case. When clients ask me how much I charge, I honestly have to tell them it does depend on the complexity of their case. Let me give you a quick example. How much does a car cost? Well, if you want a 600 series Mercedes, it is going to run $150,00. If you want an old Junker that has 100,000 miles, it's obviously a lot cheaper. Same goes with attorneys. There are three levels of pricing in a situation like yours.

If you have a super complex case that requires multiple court appearances, expert witnesses, accounting services and other professionals in addition to my services and you absolutely must have a great outcome and nothing else will do that normally runs, $15,000 to $30,000."

You want to give a range, by the way, of three to five times your normal fee. Anchor high.

Attorney: The good news, is your case isn't nearly as complicated or involved or as expensive as the top tier. Don't worry. I just like to let you know in the extreme, that's where these cases can run. Also, to put a bumper on the low end, this is where simple cases that need only the barest minimum of legal help sit. These are for people that aren't too concerned about getting a good result. They just want the cheapest, low-level legal service. Those attorneys run around $1000 or $1500 for this type of case."

Here you are telling the potential client, you already know what's out there and what they may run into. You want to defend against these cheap lawyers that are ruining your market.

Attorney: "So based on what your telling me that your single, most important need was X, Y, Z and the complexity of your case, I can tell you two good pieces of news. One, even though your case needs more than the bare minimum if you want a good result, your case isn't that complicated. Two, my rates are far less than the fancy big firms out there, but I can still accomplish a lot of work on your behalf. So instead of $15,000 to $30,000, which was the top end quote, I can handle your case for $4000. That's about 80% less or that's about $11,000 less than the super expensive guys."

As a side note, obviously, you're picking these prices, but you get the idea. Anchor high, go low. Talk about the difference. It makes it sound a lot better.

Attorney: "Do you have any questions about what I've said?"

Wait for them to answer. If they say they want to proceed then you continue:

Attorney: "Well, I'm going to email you the retainer agreement now and share it on the screen so we can go over it together. Let's go through it paragraph by paragraph and get you started. Just hold on one second. Let me get that going for you."

Share the agreement in the video chat, but also e-mail it as well.

Attorney: "Can you see the agreement on the screen now?"

Potential Client: "Yes."

Attorney: "OK, good. Check your e-mail. I sent you an agreement from DocuSign. Open it up and click to start the signature process and we'll go through everything. I'll walk you through this, so you understand everything. Let me know when you have the document open."

You pause for a minute to give the potential time to open the document.

Potential Client: "I see it. I'm ready."

Attorney: "Great. Let's get started."

Now you start going through the agreement and explaining it, paragraph by paragraph. Collect their initials as you go through each section; small positive commitments all the way through the end.

Let's say that doesn't happen. Instead, the potential raises a price objection.

Potential Client: "I can't afford it."

Or perhaps they say:

Potential Client: "I have to think about it."

Attorney: "Listen, I understand this is not a small investment for you, but it is an investment in your freedom and your peace of mind (whatever the situation may be for this client). Tell me how much of a gap there between what I quoted you and what you can pay right now. The reason I'm asking is I might be able to offer a short-term payment plan."

Here you are asking the person in a sense, "Are we far away or are we close?"

You get an idea if they are a tire kicker or if they have money to pay you. The potential client will probably say something like, "I have about half of what you're asking me for."

Note, at this point if the potential client says they have at least 30% or more of your retainer amount, you're in good shape. If they don't this is probably not going to happen.

Attorney: "Okay, so you have about a third of the total retainer. That's good. If I can offer you a payment plan where you pay X now, Y in 30 days and Z in 60 days, will that work for you?"

I personally wouldn't offer payment plans longer than the case will run, obviously and I wouldn't run them longer than six payments total with the first payment being that day. Otherwise, you are asking for trouble. That's a long time for things to go on. You want to have some runway to make sure you get paid and you don't run into a deficit on any one particular the case.

Another possible reply from the potential is if, let's say, they say instead, they have to think about it, or they need talk to someone. Well, fortunately, this means you haven't laid the groundwork properly and you haven't uncovered their true problem. Blaming someone else is not going to help you. You've got to take responsibility. Trust me. So, what do you say here?

Attorney: "Listen, I understand this is a big decision and requires a significant investment. Tell me, is there an issue with the money or is the issue related to something else?"

Then wait and let the person respond. If the person says the true problem is money go to the option above. Go through that script we just gave. If the person says it's something else, here's what you say:

Attorney: "Listen, I apologize. I take responsibility. I must not have done my job properly to inform you of everything you needed to know. I respect your decision to wait or even not to hire me at all. But so I can improve when I speak to other potential clients, tell me, what did I leave out?"

This is not an easy thing to say, but you may get good feedback. It also leaves the door open to follow up, instead of them just hanging up on you or getting crazy on you. So, if your potential client won't agree to your price and your retainer on the call, you might want to schedule for a follow up call.

Attorney: "Listen, I understand. Like I said before, I would take time to make a decision, but I really wouldn't wait more than X days because Y and Z is likely to happen. (We discussed this in the previous module). So, I have three appointment times this week and next week. I have one at 1 pm on Tuesday and on Wednesday I have a 2 pm and a 4 pm open. Which one is the best for you?"

Schedule a presumptive appointment if they are willing. You don't want to just let them get away. If you've done everything right, they at least will commit to a follow-up call. Either way, you will know if you have qualified them or you left out something critical or you weren't positioned right, because this should not happen. The sooner you can deal with the truth, the better. This is the script for price and negotiation.

CHAPTER 11

MODULE #5: THE FOLLOW UP

Module five of the *Virtual Closing System* is included with the Platinum Package, and here we cover payment plan management; how to make sure you get paid, what to do if you don't and how to get payment plans in place.

In this module we cover ways you can offer a payment plan to potential clients and yet still get paid 80% or 90% of the retainer fee upfront within 48 hours. We also talk about collections. Can you factor your receivables? Meaning, if you have money owed, can you get a lump sum discount to get cash coming in but have someone else chase your clients? If you need to stop representation early. Can you?

Module 5 also will cover managing bad reviews. All attorneys and all businesses fear them, but they are a reality. We also talk about follow up systems and why they're necessary, what they can do, how to do it properly and what that looks like. This includes how to provide leads so they can be put into the system; what's possible and why to do this in the first place. We discuss how much better can things be for you and how much more money can you make. Money lives or dies by whether you implement these things or not.

~~~~~~

Payment Plans

We will first get into payment plans. There are a few obvious recommendations that still need to be mentioned. Obviously don't give payment plans to apparent deadbeats; no matter what their promises or
~~~~~~

pleas. I think you know that. Also, don't let payment plans go on any longer than you have to. For example, with a bankruptcy client, you may have to get into six month or one-year payment plans. However, for any other area of law, a payment plan should not go longer than the case runs. Obviously, if the case finishes, you may never hear from that person again. They have zero incentive to continue paying you.

Obviously, the client has to be financially able to pay you. There is the carrot method versus the stick method. The stick method is telling the client, "I'm going to have to stop representing you if you don't pay."

You also may end up sending the client letters, notices, late fees, or even send them to collections. Chances are if you must do this, the client is going to resent you. It's not your fault, but they probably will and are much more likely to end up posting a bad review. You don't want to go down that road if you don't have to. That's why we recommend the carrot method instead, which we even have to do with our own clients sometimes.

Most of our clients pay on time but there are always going to be those who don't for whatever reason. So, the question becomes, how do you do a carrot approach instead of a stick? Let's say you offer someone a payment plan for $300 a month. What I would do, is I would let him know your payment due date is on the 15th. However, if you pay before the 15th, we will go ahead and take $20 or $30 off as a thank you for getting your payment in early.

You might be wondering why anyone would offer this to a client who is supposed to be paying you. They owe me the money. That's it. Again, however, we are using the carrot versus stick method with this approach. If you offer someone a bonus where it's even just a little bit cheaper if they pay you early, you may get 10%, 20%, 30% more clients paying you and happily doing so. Yes, you will collect a little bit less overall. However, you won't have to spend your time and resources chasing them. You won't have to lose money, time on calls, heartache, worry, and so on. You can focus on the legal work, which is what you want to do.

Implementing the carrot method, you can also send a letter congratulating the client, letting them know they have successfully completed X number of months of their payment plan.

"Congratulations Mr. Smith. You have completed three months of your six-month payment plan. You only have three payments left. As a bonus, if you want to pay your balance in full now, we will go ahead and take off $100."

Again, carrot versus stick. You get your money sooner and can focus on the legal work with confidence and ease. You are also more likely to get better reviews if you do this because your clients will feel appreciated and happy.

~~~~~~~~~~~~~~~~~~~~~~~~~~~~~~

iQualify Lending

There's a company I want to tell you about called iQualify Lending. I have known the President and CEO, Jason Brown, for about seven years now.
~~~~~~~~~~~~~~~~~~~~~~~~~~~~~~

By using their software, attorneys can iQualify Lending's software to essentially finance their clients almost immediately.

Within 48 hours, if iQualify has approved your client for a payment plan, you will then collect that first payment. Then, iQualify credits you the entire retainer minus their fee. This is a great option to offer your potentials where there are price objections. You don't have to wait for payments that may never come and chase and beg for your money. You get it almost right up front. Yes, iQualify charges a fee so you aren't getting your entire retainer in your pocket. But so what? You can easily mark-up your fees a little bit to cover that if you really want.

If you think about it, collection agencies take 30%-50% when they start chasing debtors. Additionally, they can be aggressive, and they tend to put a lot of people off. Your clients may get upset with you and end up posting bad reviews.

Now on the other hand, those companies will go to work for you if you let them and may end up being able to collect. Some collections companies do what is called factoring your receivables. Let's say you have $25,000 in payments owed to you across 18 clients. The company may agree you are owed $25,000 by your clients. However, they will pay you $17,000 and keep the rest as payment for doing the work of chasing and collecting payments.

Again, you may not be getting your full retainer. However, if you didn't go this route, you probably wouldn't have recovered anything and at least this way, you don't have to do the work of chasing the clients. In this case, at least you are able to factor your receivables, get a percentage of the money instead of nothing and move on. Sometimes that's the best.

Managing Bad Reviews

I can tell you that as many favorable client reviews as you get, there will always be the occasional bad one. It's inevitable. However, I want you to ask yourself what looks better to you? If you have a couple of bad reviews from clients but zero positive ones or you have a numerous good client reviews and only two negative ones? That's in context. Look at Amazon. Is there any product out there that has only good reviews? I'd be suspicious if it did. There's not one product or service in the world that has all positive reviews. You have to understand that and be prepared to deal with it when they do come. The solution is to insulate yourself by getting enough good reviews to insulate yourself against the bad ones.

Additionally, when it comes to any negative reviews, you should always respond but do so calmly, fairly and honestly.

Follow-Up Systems

Why is follow up necessary? I get it. You might be thinking, "I just gave this potential client my best song and dance and they didn't hire me. Why would they hire me if I follow up?"

The truth is, a lot of prospects won't necessarily make a decision to hire someone right off the bat, in any industry. Speakeasy Marketing has been in business nearly 10 years. Throughout that time, we have dealt with over 1000 clients. We are doing pretty well, but the company would be a tiny shadow of itself if we didn't follow up with potential attorney clients.

I hear from attorneys all of the time, "Rich, I've been reading your e-mails and getting your marketing materials for a year and it has me thinking."

Now, suddenly, they're ready to do something. If we didn't do any follow up with potentials, we wouldn't hear back from these people. We would have missed those opportunities.

You have to remember, everyone is busy. People forget. There are eight million things clamoring for a person's attention on a daily basis. If you don't follow up with your potential clients, you're shooting yourself in the foot. You're missing out on tens of thousands of dollars in revenue a year. Follow up is absolutely critical. It's a must.

The next thing to look at, is who should you follow up with. Of course, you always want to follow up with unconverted prospects. Those are your best bet. However, you should also follow up with past clients. Why? Because they can make referrals on your behalf or they may have additional legal needs you can assist with in an ancillary practice area.

Let's say you primarily practice family law. You have kept up with past clients through your follow up methods. A few of your past clients end up with bankruptcy issues and happen to reach out to you. If you don’t handle bankruptcy law, you could possibly refer them out to another attorney, and still get some sort of split fee. If you do handle bankruptcies, then there you go. You now have another case, courtesy of your follow up techniques.

Its true most past clients may want to forget you. You did an amazing job and got the results the client wanted and needed in their case. However, the truth is, you as their attorney, is often associated with a negative time in their life.

However, if you're showing up or following up in the right way, you can ask for positive reviews. You can get referrals or other types of cases. It just needs to be done in the proper way.

Let's say, just as an example, your main focus is criminal law. For past clients, there could be additional work such as expungements of their criminal record. For estate planning attorneys, you may have done a will for a client in the past, but the same person of a family member may need help setting up a trust in the future, or a probate matter. For family law, you might have clients who you represented in their divorce case. Now they are remarrying and want to do a prenup this time around. The point is, no matter what area of law you practice, there are always future business opportunities.

Getting back to why follow up is important, again to recap, first, when you do this properly you will retain more clients than you otherwise would. Additionally, when you follow up with past clients, you could get positive reviews they might not have otherwise thought to post. Also, again, you could also pick up additional cases with clients you have kept in touch with, depending on their current and future legal needs.

When you do proper follow up, past clients and potentials are going to associate you with a positive experience. Now they have heard from you 10 times, instead of just once when you handled their case. You will get a lot more positive reviews that way.

The next important thing to discuss regarding follow up, is how to do it effectively. How do you follow up the right way? Which practice areas will follow up work for? For example, for any type of case where an attorney was needed for an emergency or for a one-time type of situation, a lot of people think there is no point in following up. They think if the potential didn't hire me immediately, they must have moved on to hire someone else. Well, that could be true for some potentials. However, that is not necessarily true for everyone.

People often procrastinate or put off uncomfortable or unpleasant situations. Just because someone didn't hire you on day one, doesn't mean they hired someone else and that's it. They could still be waiting to retain an attorney, unsure or nervous of what to do.

There is what I call "immediate law" and "I can wait law". Immediate law is DUI and other criminal defense matters, for example. When I talk about "I can wait law", that usually would be something like a family law case. For instance, someone might be thinking about getting divorced, but they aren't acting on it right now. It could be a month or more before the potential makes a decision on whether or not to even follow through with their plans to divorce. On the other hand, with a personal injury case, the potential really can't wait to hire an attorney. There are things like statutes of limitations for filing claims. Medical bills are piling up and so on. The need to hire an attorney is more urgent. So again, if a potential hasn't hired you right away, it just may mean their need may not be urgent, or they are still thinking about who to hire. Worse yet, the potential may just be burying their head in the sand, not wanting to deal with their issue. The point is the opportunity to retain someone isn't necessarily lost if they haven't come on board immediately. If you do proper follow-up, you could still get their case. On the other hand, if you don't do any follow up, then you most certainly have lost any opportunity.

Techniques for Follow Up

Follow up needs to be done in a way where the potential or past client isn't feeling harassed. You also, of course, must ensure you are doing this following ethical standards. You also don't want to chase the person and risk losing your authority positioning. That is critical.

So, what is the best way to follow up then? I find the best way to reach out to potential clients is to do some sort of combination of e-mail, text and even some direct mail where it makes sense. You should also follow up with a phone call, send a newsletter, send a book, etcetera. All of these methods, when combined and varied, are not perceived as pestering or intrusive. Instead, following up in various ways, makes the experience for the potential richer and more meaningful. The person gets to know you better.

In a phone call, the potential hears your voice. They may get to see and experience your face expressions and your demeanor in video. If you have written a Speak A Book and have sent it to a potential, now they are experiencing your written work. They see you as an authority figure. If you have been featured in the media, send that information by email. Now they see you as an important public figure. If you have any good FAQs that would apply to a potential, share that information with them. Send them a quick email. Again, mix up the methods of contact and you are much more likely to hear back from the potentials.

Done For You Follow Up

In Module 5 of the *Virtual Closing System* we will tell you how to follow up with potential clients and with your help, we actually do some of this for you.

To make the most out of any e-mails, texts, newsletters or any other information you are sending out to potentials, the content you are sharing has to be really good. However, creating subject matter with substance takes a lot of time.

Fortunately, in Module 5, we offer you systems to help you do just this. We have prewritten content that can be customized to your specific information, including your state, practice area and so on.

I'm going to show you an example of what we do. Below is one of the e-mails in our DUI follow up series. Now, as you look at this e-mail, you can see that it's not a sales pitch. It gives the potential information and it includes some of the most frequently asked questions people have.

Sample Follow Up Email

Link To Video:

https://www.speakeasymarketinginc.com/follow-up-p2/

Yes, there is a call to action at the end but it's not a hard sell. This is a good example of what you want to use in any of the formats we mentioned. For example, if you were using this content in a text message, you may just send the headline, with a link to read the rest. If this were in an email, you have room to include the content in its entirety. If this were to be printed and mailed to the potential, again, you could send the entire thing. You could also use the content here to create a video and send it to the potential or upload to Youtube, add it to your website and so on.

As you can see, the kind of follow up I am talking about can come in many different forms. The beauty in our system, is that we can do a lot simply by using the same content in different ways, as I explained. We repurpose everything by using different parts of the text in the different delivery methods we discussed.

The next question is how often should you follow up. Should you reach out every single day? Every second day? Every third day? When should you cycle those media types? When should you call? When should you e-mail? When should you text? We answer those questions in the different protocols we use in our *Virtual Closing System*.

We have developed these methods over time and are confident we know the sequence of what works. We do follow up every single day with your potentials. However, we don't use the same media every time. We mix up the method of contacting the people on your list and also the days each item will go out. For example, let's say an email goes out to the potentials on days 1, 3, 5, 8 and 13. A phone call is made on days 7 and 11. A text phone is sent on days 7 and 11, etcetera.

The point is, we use these sequences and frequencies that are intended to gently nudge a potential to reach out to you, without pushing them away. Of course, there is always the thought that you don’t want to be a bother to someone. There's always the natural fear of getting a nasty reply from a potential demanding you take them off your contact list or something like that. I get them all the time and so will you. If you are going to follow up with people, you can't just run and hide if this happens.

My team at Speakeasy emails our potentials maybe six days out of the week. With that frequency, we always get a few responses calling us scammers or spammers or better yet to “F” off. Luckily for the few negative responses we get, there are many more positive. In the same day we are told our approach is wrong, we get another email right behind that saying, “Rich, thank you so much for your e-mail. It's awesome. Can we work together?”

I see these types of responses side by side all of the time. I used to feel bad when I would get people cursing me out. Now I just crack up laughing. More often than not, the responses we get from our outreach are people thanking us for the information. Some people have even told us they were brought to tears and that we saved their practice. When that happens, it emboldens me to keep going.

When you do get those negative responses just simply respond, "No problem, sir. No problem, ma'am. We'll take you off our list. Have a nice day."

Usually people are not going to go crazy on you and try to get you in trouble for following up. Just have a protocol in place.

A simple, "We will take you off the list right away," will do. That's the best you can do. You have to have a little bit of thick skin and not let it bother you. You are doing yourself tremendous good by following up with potentials. If you don't, you are going to have a lot less revenue and you are losing out on helping those people. What you do is valuable. You're doing people a disservice by not giving them at least a few shots to work with you.

If you don't actively and accurately catalog who is calling you, who you are pitching on initial consults and what their responses are, you're not going to know who to follow up with or how. You must have a designated person in your office to collect this information; whether that's you, your secretary, your partner, or whoever that may be. Someone has to be designated to do this task. That person should have a template to record every single lead that comes in by email, phone, chat, whatever it is. The template should include a place to record the potential's name, email, phone number, type of case and any specifics that will help you, the attorney, get back to them with a tailored message. You should be receiving these reports every single day and the information should be recorded in your follow up system.

This is where we take over. We have set up a page, which we call the "411" page. Of course, 411 is what you dial for information on the telephone, or at least it used to be. Now we just Google everything.

At any rate, this page can exist on your website, on a hidden page, or we can host it for you. Here you enter a first name, last name, email, phone number, the practice area and any special notes. Then you just click and hit enter. Now that person's information goes into our system and we do the follow up for you. We start sending the e-mails and the texts and we prompt you to do the follow-up phone calls and any other methods you want to include. It makes the job of following up a lot easier. We can't do it without your help, of course. You have to at least give us the information from your designated person and give it to us often. Then when we do the follow up for you, we give you the report.

The report will have details including who is opening the emails, who opened just one e-mail, only two weeks ago. It will tell you who is getting your text messages and whether they are responding.

We also give you a list of the hottest to the coldest. Guess who you should follow up with first? The hottest, of course. We'll let you know these people are ready. These people are still percolating, so once you have this report you know who to follow up with immediately and when. You know who to let sit in the oven and cook a little longer.

This is what you want for your follow up system. This shouldn't be time consuming, but having this protocol is critical and it's worth it. With our help, you will have a great follow up pipeline. You are going to see a lot more retainers and your business is going to grow.

So, what's possible? I used to run a website where we provided DUI leads nationwide. It was called myduiattorney.org and we delivered about 35,000 DUI leads to attorneys all over the United States. We saw the best and the worst. There were some attorneys that were so bad, if you stapled the lead to them, they couldn't convert it. These people usually would complain that the reason they weren't closing deals was because the leads were bad. Truthfully, it was their fault. We know this, because we had other attorneys who were getting leads and they were converting at least 30% of what we sent them, and they loved our service. Now this was without any additional follow up systems. That 30% conversion was just coming from the cold, raw ability of these attorneys to do consults, pitch people, get them in and close them.

With the follow up system I've been explaining to you, we can do far better than that 30 percent. You will probably never get to the point of converting 100% of all potentials you connect with. You may not even get to 70%. However, if you start closing close to 40% percent, maybe even 55% of the potential clients you interact with, that's probably a huge increase for you. This could mean doubling or tripling revenue for some people. So, forget getting to 100% when it comes to closing clients. Who cares? We'll never get you there. However, we can improve your position radically and get you a lot more money each month. That's what's possible with the proper follow up system. This is realistic and it doesn't matter the practice area.

Now that you've seen the basics of this module, get in touch with us. We will get the 411-

page set up. You will have your designated person start sending us your potential clients and we're going to do the follow up and send you reports. Once you have that invaluable information, you must read those reports, do the additional follow up and convert those potentials.

CHAPTER 12

BONUS MODULE #6: IQUALIFY LENDING WITH JASON BROWN

I'm going to call the next part of this book the Bonus Module or Module 6. When I first came up with the *Virtual Closing System*, I would mention iQualify Lending as a suggestion to attorneys for a way to offer their clients payment plans. However, the more I thought about it, the more I wanted to make this a permanent part of the *Virtual Closing System*. So I decided to talk to one of the owners of iQualify and he was all for it. Now, I assure you, I don't get any money from them for doing this. I have simply decided to include their services in our VCS because I think it's important and I know it can be a useful tool for you.

Up to this point, the whole goal here has been to help you retain a higher percentage of clients. However, there are still going to be clients that say they want to think about it and costs may be in the back of their mind. If you can do anything to remove at least one barrier hiring you, why wouldn't you and iQualify Lending can do that.

I am going to share with you a conversation I had with Jason Brown of iQualify Lending.

Richard Jacobs: Jason, you mentioned a statistic of the attorneys that are using iQualify Lending. How many more clients, would you say, as a percentage, are they retaining now?

Jason Brown: I would say it's about 47%.

Richard Jacobs: One of the first things attorneys always want to know is if iQualify Lending will work for their practice or the type of law they practice. So what type of attorneys have you worked with the most?

Jason Brown: I'd say our three most prominent fields are going to be criminal defense, family law and immigration law.

Richard Jacobs: What about bankruptcy? As the state sets the fees, I don't know if that applies here.

Jason Brown: Keeping in mind, one of the aspects of what we offer is a financial product. We have a product where you can literally do financing on a legal retainer fee. With bankruptcy, we tend to find that those people are more credit challenged and the product doesn't work as well in that field. However, again, it does work incredibly well with criminal defense, family and immigration attorneys.

Richard Jacobs: How about estate planning?

Jason Brown: Oh, sure. Absolutely!

Richard Jacobs: And then, any civil type cases that may work as well. Right?

Jason Brown: I mean, really, we can handle just about any type of law. But we find that the highest and best use attorneys are those in those three fields. Again though, if you do business planning, if you work with clients on trademarks or just about anyone you can think of, we can lend to. We have found, however, that the type of law that produces higher caseloads or consistent workflow coming in and people that need you to meet them where they are financially, do exist primarily in those three areas.

Richard Jacobs: How long have you been providing loans for attorneys?

Jason Brown: We're heading on five years. We created this product and many different iterations of it along the way. We worked with the state bars along the way to get their approval and find a way that was going to work legally. In the past six months, we actually were able to work with the American Bar Association to get them to write an opinion about what we've done favorably. They've endorsed us. So now we work in all 50 states and we have attorneys in 47 states.

Richard Jacobs: That's great. Okay. So, it's bar compliant pretty much in every state, right?

Jason Brown: Yes and, we gave offers to $357 million in fees last year.

Richard Jacobs: Okay, that's excellent. I know attorneys are concerned about the ethics of this so being approved by the ABA is great. What's the very basic parameters of what you do? Let's say I'm an attorney and I have a client. I'm doing my initial consult. Now it comes to the point of money. Let's say I charge $5000 for a retainer. Normally, I would say my fee is $5000 but maybe I can take half of it now and half in a month. As the attorney, what can I do with your system and how can that be improved?

Jason Brown: Sure. So our system has three steps. We did a survey and Cleo also did a survey that agreed with our survey. The results said that 63% of clients who meet with an attorney leave feeling confused or unsure about the next steps and how to pay for the case. That's why we really have focused in on the closing. Attorneys want to convert more clients. They want to make more money and they want to stop chasing their clients for money. So, our system is primarily developed to solve those issues. We provide a cash option. When you apply or when you're speaking with a client and you want to present the payment options, what we've done is kind of modeled that of the dental and medical industry. We're going to present you three payment options. Here's your cash option of $5000. We have a financing option that you could choose. That would be zero down. You could pay the loan back over time with a fixed investment or a fixed interest rate loan, just like a car payment and that would be about $150 a month. If neither of those options would work, we could work something out in-house where we'd take $2500 down payments of $450 or $500 a month over the next couple of months and we can work it out that way.

By giving a client all three options right then and there, it meets the client where they are financially and allows them to say yes more, which is why our attorneys are converting so many more clients than the average attorney, as we're giving your client that opportunity to say yes, right then and there and essentially, that's what you're looking for. You want more yes and less let me think about it.

Richard Jacobs: That's the bane of everyone's existence. So what if the potential client tells the attorney he needs to think about it? Or some other excuse. I know attorneys don't want to chase those people. They feel icky about doing it like they're annoying the person. So you want to get it right there on that call. That's the whole goal of this Virtual Closing System and that's why I brought you in here to talk about this.

Jason Brown: I think the parts and pieces of your system and our system line up perfectly. When the attorney has done their three-part presentation, the client is closed on the competency of the attorney. It really just does become can they afford it? And when you give that client all three options, it feels more like a banking product now. Whether they choose to pay upfront or take a financing option, or they choose a payment plan, it looks, acts and feels like a bank. It removes some of that ickiness and some of the responsibility on the attorney. Now it's a banking product instead of an attorney product, if you will.

Richard Jacobs: What I like, is it separates the attorney's representation completely from the money side.

Jason Brown: Correct.

Richard Jacobs: The attorney says, "All right. Here's the financing available". The person takes it. The attorney gets paid, in full, minus the small fee.

Jason Brown: Yeah, it's a 5% fee.

Richard Jacobs: Here is why it's important for people to know. The attorney gets paid in full pretty soon, usually within a couple of days. That way, they can focus on the legal work, which is what they want to do. They don't have to worry about the money. Then if the client stops paying, they don't have to try to get themselves out of the case. They can just do the legal work they've been paid for. If the client doesn't pay, that's handled with the bank; with the finance company. That has nothing to do with the attorney. It keeps the person emotionally separated from the two. It doesn't lead to bad reviews. It doesn't lead to being upset at the attorney or any of that. That's why I think it's awesome. I wanted to point that out.

Jason Brown: Right. I agree with you. Remove the emotional component of collecting money. I tell this kind of joke often that you can graduate from Harvard or Brown or Princeton. You can get a 180 on your ELSA. You hang your shingle. You're ready to be an attorney and you sign your first client. All of a sudden, you're a collection agent. Nobody came out of law school thinking, "Oh, man, I can't wait to be a collections agent when I grow up." They wanted to be an attorney. Our system allows you to practice law and we handle everything else financially. No calling clients. No chasing them around. Like you said, it's getting funded in full, upfront with no recourse and that's a really big deal. When the loan is funded to the attorney, they don't have to worry about me coming back and saying, "Hey, the client didn't pay. You owe me money."

We take all of the risk in full upfront and we're doing it with 12 different lenders in our platform. This means that you're going to get as many options as humanly possible for a client to be able to pay you. The client gets to choose the best deal for them and the attorney walks away smelling like roses because you just took a $5000 DUI zero down, $150 fixed installment loan, just like a CARNO and the client can afford it. They get access to justice. The attorney got paid in full and many fees, it's earned upon receipt. It's immediately available and it really solves the problem of cash flow, liquidity.

Richard Jacobs: Excellent. You mentioned this a bunch of times. Attorneys tend to think of financing as a last resort only if the person says, "I don't have money," or "I can't afford it", but you've also told me in private conversations that the attorneys that are doing the best are offering it to everyone. Why would they do that?

Jason Brown: I think there's a mindset issue that is natural. If we go back to the story of hanging your shingle and all of a sudden becoming a collection agent, I think attorneys are primed against wanting to put someone on a payment plan because it makes them a collection agent. They want to get paid cash right now, today. Many attorneys have cash flow issues, month to month. They have to pay their bills so everyone wants to get paid in cash. Having dealt with thousands of attorneys, we realize that doesn't happen. It maybe happens 10% of the time, where a client can really pay in full upfront and some practices are built differently. The reality is, getting paid in full, upfront is important. If you only offer financing to clients who don't have a job, they don't have another way to pay you. You wouldn't put them on a payment plan. There's no way we're going to get them approved for financing. Attorneys, I think, had that mentality of like as a last resort, they would offer financing. Financing can be complicated to an attorney. It's why we built the system that presents all three options at once. It takes the attorney out of the conversation. It makes it very clear this is how clients are used to doing business. They are used to going and being offered a cash price. They're used to going and being offered a financing price. The only difference for them is that you will work on an in-house payment plan with them as well, by us managing that for you. It takes away that headache for the attorney. I think offering financing to everyone upfront is important because oftentimes people with great credit are going to want to finance a product. They're used to doing it that way.

Richard Jacobs: There's a couple things I know attorneys get into, one being they hate low ballers. Let's say if a DUI is normally $5000, some attorneys might say they will do it for $1500. The good attorneys know that the low-ball attorney is going to barely do any legal work. They'll just plead the person out, for instance. They have to defend against those people because some clients call and say, "Oh, so-and-so will do it for $1500."

Well, what you guys offer can take all that away. You could say, "Not only can I do a lot more for the amount of money I'm charging, but if I only charge you $1500, I could barely represent you. There's not much I could do. I could have multiple appearances in court. I couldn't get expert witnesses, etc. So, not only does my fee allow me to do a lot more for you, but we have payment plans that actually will be more affordable than shelling out that $1500 to so-and-so."

I can see that this would be a really great antidote to those low ballers that are out there in the market and it would still keep the attorneys positioning and value.

Jason Brown: If you pair it with the system that you've built, it's one of the things that I really like. With your virtual close system, the attorney can go through everything with the client and show them the difference in what they get based on what they pay. Going through the case details and drawing out the diagram and having that outcome tree allows the client to see the difference in what they are getting for their money. You and I and every attorney in the world knows one thing's for sure. People believe that most people with money don't face the same kind of criminal justice issues or family issues that people without money face. People with money want an affordable way to hire an expert to help them with their case. Your system shows that the attorney is an expert. My system gives them the affordable way to do that and it's the perfect pairing.

Richard Jacobs: I want to talk about the types of clients that attorneys would take on, too. If you only offer financing or payment plans to people that tell you they have no money, they're not likely to be a good client. They're telling you they have no money. So even on a payment plan, they probably wouldn't be able to pay you or they'll fall out. In addition, emotionally, those kinds of people tend to have other problems in their life; maybe fault of their own, no fault of their own. But everyone knows that a stressed, anxious and unhappy client in their own personal life, comes back on you as the attorney. They'll call you more often in desperation. They may end up getting arrested while you're in the middle of representation or a domestic violence call or having to file bankruptcy or who knows.

They tend not to make good clients at all. So, you want to offer financing to people that are emotionally resilient and have some ability to function normally. The financing does this and it doesn't just give the person the money. It also relaxes them because the financial burden on the client is less. Now, the client can be better behaved because they have less of a money pressure in their own life. They haven't had to shell out $2000, $3000, $5000 or $10,000 in one big nut. It's a lot of stress for them so they will be a better-behaved client for you just because of that.

Jason Brown: I agree completely. I mean, J. Bloomberg said it best. He said that a client that can't or won't pay you at the beginning of the case, can't and won't pay you at the end of the case. Clients without money are always going to be without money. What our system does though, is it changes that prospect of having money. Not everyone has $10,000 sitting in a 401(k) and their savings account to be able to stroke a check. Most people don't. As a matter of fact, statistically, we know that 70% of America or north of 60% of America, is one paycheck away from being out on the streets. What we have learned, is that if I can make your legal case about the same cost as a family cell phone plan, you're talking about adding tremendous value to a client's life at that point in time.

You have a grateful client; someone who is going to tell everyone they know about you. That word of mouth, again, is going to drive more free business through your front door. Just by providing a solution for your client, because not every attorney has it. And when you do it, you have a significant leg up.

Richard Jacobs: I recently had a fence put in around my house and I had the same situation. We had a finance company that we pay. I feel about completely differently about them, then I feel about my fence guy. My fence guy did a good job. I love him. I even called him the other day to refer him. The finance company, I don't like because them, I have to pay. I realized I'm experiencing the same thing. It's completely separate from the fence guy in my mind. So, I imagine that the same thing happens with the attorney is that the client will be very happy with the attorney. They can focus on the legal side and the finance stuff, is someone else's game. There is no ill will that leaks over to the attorney from it.

Jason Brown: Exactly. It's a very simple psychological hack that is incredibly effective. We look, act and feel like a bank. The clients make their payments to us because of that. There aren't the sob stories and like you've mentioned the kind of the emotional turmoil that many clients are going through in events like this. Oftentimes the attorney becomes the therapist and the psychiatrist, having to walk through all of that. Then they've heard all of this information and now they to ask him for money, knowing about their situation. It makes for a very uncomfortable situation for the attorney. Attorneys manage their own payment plans. They are collection agents. They do take money upfront for cases. However, then they are also acting as a business owner. For example, if they get a notification that one of their client's payments didn't go through, that makes them stop in their tracks. Then the attorney has to stop what he's doing and go assess if he needs to call the client. He has to look at how much they owe and if they are behind. He needs to look at if the client has a court date coming up. Does he need to petition the judge to be withdrawn from the case? He has to then chase these people down with 15 telephone calls or have his admin do it. This happens multiple times a day to every attorney in America. It's a nightmare to manage that aspect of it. Imagine getting an e-mail that says your client has charged back the $4000 fee and the bank withdraws it from your account immediately. Imagine not having to deal with that. Imagine not having to get those e-mails that say our client missed a payment plan. Somebody else can take care of that for you.

Matter of fact, we do it so well that our attorneys typically make 93 cents on the dollars for their cases that are on payment plans with us. Now, if your firm is making that kind of money, you don't need me right now. If you're not near ninety-three cents, imagine what life looks like if you just got paid more for the clients you already are signing. This isn't rocket science here. We're just better at it than you are. That's it.

Richard Jacobs: Let's get into some of the parameters. I know it depends on the person's finances, but what are the loan amounts that you go up to and what's the interest rate?

Jason Brown: I'll just kind of give you a general outline. It's loan amounts from $1000 to $50,000. Decisions are made instantly. A client can apply without affecting their credit. That's what's called a soft credit pull and our interest rates follow federal usury rates for credit card guidelines, which annotate that we can charge between 2.99% and 29.99% interest. Those rates will be based on your credit, the length of the term and the type of loan that you take. The beauty is, that we have a large bank of lenders that are all competing for the right to earn your client's business. You're not just stuck with whatever offer you get. Oftentimes, our clients will receive multiple offers and from different lenders which allow them to find the deal that's the best fit for them while the attorney gets paid in full upfront.

Richard Jacobs: The loan terms are what? Two to five years?

Jason Brown: Yes, two to five years. That's correct. One of the things I do want to touch on that we built in specifically because we work with attorneys is, we remove the headache of wondering how much they would qualify for. So let's say you have a divorce case and you need $10,000 as your retainer up front and a client applies for financing. If they couldn't get approved for the entire $10,000, we have an automated counteroffer system built in. It would tell you the client is a go, could get approved for up to $7500 so that you don't have to wonder, and keep applying and try and hit the nail on the head with what you could get a yes on. Inversely, let's say it's a family case and you apply for $10,000, but they got approved for up to $20,000 or $25,000. That allows you to have a realistic conversation with the client right then and there about the potential future cost of the case and how they intend to pay for that. You may be able to gather all of the money upfront because the client knows that they could take a $20,000 loan for $600 a month.

Richard Jacobs: What that also tells you is the way it reveals the hand of your client. It tells you how financially strong they are. Again, this goes back to a good client versus a pain in the ass client. A good one is going to be financially stable enough and have less problems.

Jason Brown: Right and many attorneys, I'm sure, are going to find that to be true.

Richard Jacobs: Let's go through everything. Let's start with the application process. I'm on the phone or I'm on video with a potential client and we get to that point of talking about the retainer. I give him the three options like you said, the person says, financing, what do I do? How do I apply? What are the steps literally from that point?

Jason Brown: If they want to apply for financing, when you create those three options to talk about with the client, there's a button on there that you can say e-mail to client. That way they get it in real time and from that email they can apply for financing or go onto a payment plan from anywhere; from their phone, from their computer. If, however, you are sitting with a client right then and there and they say they want to apply for financing, it's a 30 second application. They would click submit and in about 15 seconds they will get offers from all of the banks. The attorney will also get an email with all of the offers that we made to the client. That way, if a client applies later in the evening when they thought they might take a payment plan, but they decided to go financing instead just to see if they get approved, the attorney will know what they were approved for.

It will not affect the client's credit to apply and see what offers they have. They will be notified which lenders made those offers. They click accept offer. The bank reaches out, or we reach out and within 24 to 72 hours, that client is funded. The attorney is notified that they can be paid in full and the client goes on a payment plan that starts in 30 days.

Richard Jacobs: So, as the attorney during the initial consult, when we get to the point where the client applies and they get offers, am I safe to go ahead now and present my retainer agreement and move forward?

Jason Brown: I would. Matter of fact, most of our attorneys are going to add some kind of contingent to language just for this. Because if, for example, we make them an offer, and for some reason they can't prove their income like maybe they worked as a bartender and make all tips but they told us they made $50,000 a year, and now they can't prove it, those kinds of things could get in the way. It doesn't happen often, but by having that contingent to retainer financing agreement in your general language, that will allow you to say if you are taking a loan to pay for the value of this case and you do not receive the funds for the loan, then this retainer is null and void.

Richard Jacobs: Oh, good. Right because you don't want to get trapped in a case and have the judge not let you out.

Jason Brown: What most attorneys are doing, is they are telling the clients once they are approved for financing that they can then go ahead and sign the retainer agreement. They could even take a small deposit if they want. We don't require that but it could be a handshake that closes the deal with your client. They've paid you money. They've signed an agreement. They're your client now. So if you ever had a client take financing and the money and then back out, that was just because you didn't do a good job closing them; having them sign the agreement, getting them as a client for you. I don't think any of the clients that are using this video closing system are going to have that issue because they've clearly established their value and now, they're just waiting on payment.

Richard Jacobs: You do want to take a token amount, even if it's a $100 or something. That makes it okay. This is serious. We're doing this, this is your good faith deposit to me.

Jason Brown: Most people won't shake your hand on an agreement and then back out. It's just naturally how we're built.

Richard Jacobs: Again, I encourage the attorneys to take a token amount of something just to seal the deal. So the person gets the offers, then they do the paperwork with the lenders directly and then typically, how long does it take for that person to get their paperwork in? And then what happens once they do?

Jason Brown: Again, you're looking at 24 to 72 hours from the time that the client reaches out to the bank and accepts this offer. That's when the underwriters and the processors get involved and make sure that if we need a pay stub or a bill to verify their address, we will go ahead and procure that on behalf of the client. We do all of the work and then once the loan is ready to fund and funds are disbursed, the client and the attorney will get an email that tells them the loan has been funded. Then it's time to collect your fee. Once that happens, the attorney reaches back out to the client and says, "Congratulations! Everything is good to go ahead and pay up the remainder of the balance. So $5000 minus the $500 I took upfront. That'll be $4500. The client makes the payment to the attorney and then the client makes the payments to the lender again, first payment due in 30 days."

Richard Jacobs: There is one thing that I want to clarify. Because of the bar rules and ethics, the loan money will actually get deposited to the client's account first and then the attorney drafts it from there. You recommend going through ACH. They set that up beforehand. This is how the ABA, and everyone wanted it set up. So, the money or the loan will go into the client's account. It gets drafted right away to your account and you'll get notified. Now you've got your money. Great. Now you just start as normal with the client and you don't have to worry about anything. The client will start getting their bills from the financing company and off you go. Super simple. That's great.

I want to talk now about some of the mechanics of the system for attorneys to use it. What does it cost them? And each time they do a loan, what does it cost, etc.? Let's go into that.

Jason Brown: The cost to the system that we charge is $2.99 per month; that's every month. We charge a one-time $299 set up. In addition to that, we charge a 5% fee, regardless of whether it's financing or an in-house payment plan that we're managing for the attorney. It's 5% of whatever is collected. So, if a client actually needed to pay an attorney $5000, but they got approved and funded for $10,000 and the attorney only collects his fee, we're only going to make them pay the 5% fee on whatever money they received from the client, from the proceeds.

Richard Jacobs: So, for a given loan, it's $50 per $1000 fee that the attorney would pay. So, if they do a $5000 retainer, they're going to pay, $250 in fees to use the net.

Jason Brown: Right. In some states, you're required to charge that fee to the client. For example, Texas requires that you charge that 5% fee to the client. You'll receive the five thousand plus the $250 to cover that fee. You can choose to markup your fees if you want to; if it's allowed in your state. We will tell you when you come in what the rules are for your state and then again, with the payment plan, if we manage one of those for you. Again, if I collect $100 payment I keep $5, give $95 back to you. Those are the costs associated with using the system. If somebody does go on a payment plan with us, the client will actually pay a $49 one-time setup fee and we just ping that against their bank account or their payment method to establish that payment.

Richard Jacobs: So, the attorney keeps 95% of the retainer. That's incredibly reasonable in my mind. If you're going to fight over the 5%, that means you're pricing yourself so close to the bone that you're not going to be in business anyway. So, 5% really is not going to hurt anybody. You mentioned estate planning in the beginning and that those attorneys close to 47% more clients. The fees to do this are minimal. If you use this system and you're closing one more case every month because of this, it more than pays for itself. So, the fees seem really minimal to me.

Jason Brown: Oddly enough, we don't charge enough, really. We could charge an extra 10% and people would still pay us once they see the results. To your point, if you get two clients a month approved for financing, that's $120,000 in additional upfront immediate cash revenue. That's a boatload of money for a small firm where two finance loans would make a really big difference. The other thing to keep in mind is if you are pricing yourself close to the bone where profit margins are slim, start thinking about your case costs in terms of monthly dollars. For example, if you did a $1000 case, it's $30 a month. If you start applying that mentality to what, a $5000 case that's $150 a month. A $6000 case is only $80 a month. When you start thinking about it like that, think about if you raised your fee by $1000, could the client sitting in front of you afford an extra $25 or $30 a month?

Richard Jacobs: That's what's really cool. Maybe a good example is selling a car. Let's say I'm talking to a client and the potential client wants to work with me. I tell him the fee and what the payments are. If they agree, then you could maybe tell them if they can handle a little bit more in payments and they are approved for more, you can use that to call in extra witnesses or you can do more appearances for them and so on. You could let the client know that you could do a lot more work and would most likely get a better result.

Jason Brown: Right and that goes into what you call your decision tree in the Virtual Close System. My first question, if I were an attorney, would be what specific outcome would-be best-case scenario in the matter that we're talking about right now? Because when you talk about it in those regards, you've got them thinking about solving the problem, not dealing with it.

Richard Jacobs: I always tell the attorneys to ask the client what the most important thing about their situation is that they want resolved above everything else. I tell them to keep harping on that because it aligns perfectly with what the person just told the attorney. If you give that to them or if you keep refocusing on whatever is important to them, they are going to want to proceed.

Jason Brown: Absolutely. So, again, once you get someone talking about solving the case now, cost is not the issue. Now, affordability is the issue. I don't care what it costs me. The question is, can I afford it? So as the client, if I'm thinking about a $5000 DUI case at $150 a month, when you tell me you could bring in expert witnesses and really go after the DA and it's only going to cost me an extra $2000, which is only $60 a month for me, that seems worth it. You're talking about freedom for an extra $60 a month. This could mean not losing my license. Not going to jail and I won't have to do community service. You know what I mean? I know you can't promise an outcome, but I'm just thinking about the possibility of the things that you could do for an extra $30 a month and a $1000 to the attorney.

Richard Jacobs: It's a good exercise for any attorney. For example, if you're family law, what does that look like for you? Can you tell the person, "You know what, we might be able to get a better parenting plan for you; get you more visitation and more co-parenting."

If it's an estate situation the attorney might say, "We may be able to mount a much better defense in that the other beneficiaries don't take the house and you get nothing."

If it's a criminal case, where the client is looking at maybe a long time in jail, you could say, "Now we have the money to maybe make an appeal or two and really see if we can keep you out of jail or reduce your time."

For any attorney, think about your particular practice area and then imagine what could you do for a client if they paid you a couple of thousand more or maybe even five thousand more in some cases and that will get you going. Then you can see how that only costs the client another $30 a month per $1000 and that's great.

Jason Brown: Also, keep in mind, is there's what I call the "car conundrum". Everyone who owns a car thinks that people would not ever pay more than they're paying a month. If you're paying $400 a month, you might be thinking that no one pays $600 or $800 a month for a car. Well, a large percentage of America does. You would be surprised at what people can afford. See, that's the difference. When you want me to write you a check for $20,000, I don't have it. However, I can take $600 a month in debt and afford it. That's the mentality that has to change with attorneys and anyone who is reading this. You have to stop thinking about this in terms of, "How many zeros can I collect?"

Instead you need to think, "What monthly payment could these people afford and what fee could I charge for that?"

Richard Jacobs: That's how I think about it too. "Oh, it's only another $100 a month. I'll figure it out."

Jason Brown: Oddly enough, it's the American way. It's interesting, as we've all been in a situation where if we had just done a little bit more, the outcome would have been extraordinarily different. That's how I think about it. If I'm speaking with an attorney and he gives me the option to pay $60 more a month to do all of these extra things that could make a serious difference in my case and I said no, I would live with serious regret. Nobody's going to say no, if they can afford it. I mean that's really where you find out what people can really afford.

Richard Jacobs: How long does it take to get set up and how do attorneys find you?

Jason Brown: Go to iqualifylending.com. Fill out one of the many forms that are on our website. You will get an e-mail to book a time with one of our sales specialists. They will reach out and have a conversation with you. They will answer any questions you may have on how the system works. From there, you give us a little bit of information about your firm and within 24 hours, we've got you up and running. You could be offering financing tomorrow if you start today.

Richard Jacobs: I also wanted to talk about the other products you offer as well. I I'm an attorney and I already have a book of receivables of say, 30 clients on a payment plan, can you help me to collect from those people? What can you do in that situation?

Jason Brown: We can. It's reformatting one of the products that we have right now, which is part of our three-part offer system. We built a system after having financing for three years and having good success with it. However, we realized we still hadn't solved the problem for attorneys of getting paid because not everybody gets approved for financing and not everybody who gets approved for financing, takes the offer. When that happens attorneys would freak themselves out and put somebody on a payment plan. As a result of that, we realized attorneys were still putting 40% to 60% of their clients on payment plans. So we solved that problem by building a system that manages payment plans, collects on their behalf and sets up a way to actually charge an interest rate if the state allows it.

We partnered with a company that is backed by Dan Gilbert at Rocket Mortgage. Dan helped us create a banking compliance product that allows us to manage the payment plans for attorneys. You put a client on a payment plan. We manage it from contract set up, every payment call and follow up. If there's a collection we handle that as well. Lots of attorneys are taking payments from clients and have Social Security numbers and credit card numbers on Excel spreadsheets. It is a wildfire waiting for an ignition switch. It's really unhealthy for that to happen.

Richard Jacobs: What's the consequence if an attorney has that kind of private data and something happens? Could the attorney be liable?

Jason Brown: I've seen it in attorneys' offices where there's an Excel spreadsheet with all of the client's information, bank account numbers, credit card numbers and Social Security numbers. If an attorney gets hacked, and all it takes is someone with a camera and bad intention, or someone could literally just come in and take a picture, you can say goodbye to your law practice. It takes you out the door.

The reality is, when it comes to money, you need to have someone who is a professional banker. You need people who understand SOC-2 security and how to build all of this technology and pass it through and not leave a digital footprint. That in and of itself is where the feds get involved. The SEC comes knocking on your door and that's not what you want.

Richard Jacobs: You said a lot of attorneys will have a big book or receivables. How can they hand that book to you and you manage it? What's involved?

Jason Brown: I give this example all the time. Let's say a client owes you $2500 and you're trying to collect $500 a month from them. It's not going to happen. But if you call back and said, "Hey, can you pay me $120 a month?", now what you've done is you've made a reasonable offer. This is something that most people can say yes to and for you, it's already charged off debt. If the client says yes and you put them on a payment plan and I manage it for you, really what you've done is you've turned your charge offs and your collectibles into mailbox money until that debt's paid for. Once we're done with that cycle, imagine not having collectable debt anymore.

Imagine not having to deal with that, because if you're left with a book of business with us, we can literally renegotiate the contract on your behalf at any point in time. If the client says, “Listen, my wife lost her job and we can't make a $500 payment,” if we can respond and ask the client if they can make a smaller payment, say just $150 a month, now you are collecting something. Of course, those are the things that we have to work with the attorneys on and get their okay with. But this is something we have the ability to do for an attorney. We already know that things are going to happen and it's our job to try and not involve the attorney in any way, shape or form unless we have to. If a client is 60 days delinquent and they aren't making payments, I do have to notify the attorney and say, “Listen. It's time for you to petition the judge and see if you can get removed from the case for nonpayment.”

If you're in a situation where the judge says you're stuck on the case, we renegotiate the monthly fee. Most attorneys would rather collect $100 from somebody than nothing if the judge is going to bind them to the case. You have to meet the clients where they're at financially and when we do that, everybody gets paid.

Richard Jacobs: The other dimension is that there's an emotional part to collections; a personnel part. You need a body to sit there, pick up the phone and call and e-mail these people, get information, write it down and run the cards. Often you need your admins to do that. If you're a true solo, you do it yourself, but it sucks up your time. An attorney who has to worry about processing payments can't be filing motions and focusing on the legal side of things if they're caught up in the collections part. If you hate collections, you know your admins aren't going to want to do it. They may even feel bad for your clients and not even try that hard to collect. That happens all of the time. A lot of attorneys are perceived as rich, even if they're not, and the clients are perceived as the poor person that just needs help. So, you may be getting sabotaged by your admins and never know it.

Jason Brown: Exactly, “Karen”, who works at the front, didn't realize that a large percentage of her life was going to be devoted to chasing down clients for money like shakedown Fridays. She didn't realize that was part of the job but she does the work. She likes you. She likes the family feel of the law firm. But Karen is also a mother and so she hears these stories, and has a natural empathy for who she talks to. To your point, this person is going through a tough time and “Karen” has been sitting on the phone for 45 minutes listening to them. Then she is coming back and selling you on why she can't collect the payment.

It's a double loss for you as a solo practitioner or a small firm. If we can take “Karen” out of that process completely, then we remove the stress from her and from you. We give you her time back. She can focus on things that are actually going to help you, so you win more cases and achieve better results for your clients. Fixing the problem for “Karen” as well as for you is so important and is a much bigger problem than you think it is. I promise you. I'll tell you a quick story. We were talking to one of the largest criminal defense firms out on the West Coast who have done financing with us for years. They make about $100,000 a month in financing. They found out that we created this back-end product to manage payment plans and when we reached out to them and told them we had it, we immediately had all of the owners on the phone. It took 15 minutes. It's a massive problem for them. Who is managing it? What if someone calls in sick? What if somebody takes maternity leave or quits or gets fired? Then you have to teach someone how to do all of this. Get them all back up today. Get everybody back online and there's a really good chance you might go weeks without collecting payment unless you're going to do it yourself again. Now we're back to that whole collection agent thing. So, when they found that out that we could do this for them, they got paper burn trying to sign the agreement. They signed up immediately. This was a problem they never wanted to have to manage again. Now they can't imagine their life doing that work again. Imagine never having to worry about calling and chasing clients around for money again. Think about how that would feel if that problem just disappeared from your practice today.

What we've done is to wrap it all up. It was us and CLEO that both came to the same conclusion. We found that 63% of the time a client leaves your office feeling unsure about the next steps and how to pay for the case. We offer clarity on those three options. We meet the clients where they are and that allows the attorneys to convert more clients and make more money. They are happier because they're not doing shakedown Fridays and chasing their clients for money.

Richard Jacobs: Excellent and again, how do attorneys reach you? What's the best way?

Jason Brown: Go to iqualifylending.com and fill out the form. A salesperson will reach out. It's a super quick process. If you reached out today, we could have you signed up and ready to go by tomorrow.

CHAPTER 14

WHAT IS THE VIRTUAL CLOSING SYSTEM WORTH TO YOU?

This program is an investment. It's not an expense. The price is not very high. It's geared so that if you get one client ever for the rest of your life because of it, you have paid for it.

If you don't prosper using this system, then there is something clearly wrong. It just means you are not using it, frankly. I honestly cannot see any way that you can't earn your investment back plus multiples. I believe in this system.

I am going to give you a low average here, but let's say since you started applying the tactics you learned in the *Virtual Closing System,* you are now getting two to three new cases a month that you otherwise would have gone to a competitor. Let's also say, your average case is worth $3000 to you.

That means the *Virtual Closing System* is worth $108,000 of cash per year or $9000 per month based on these fair estimates. I'm not promising you the moon. I'm not saying it's going to be a flood of new cases right away. However, I think this is very reasonable approximation. This doesn't even take into account the time you save driving to meet a client, the time you waste on no shows and the time you spend talking to potentials that are not going to turn into new clients.

Questions & Answers

Q. Hey Rich, I've been following you for a while. I love your stuff. Do you do video meetings yourself?

A. Our sales meetings are often done now through Zoom. Our main salesperson's closing rate has gone up a lot since using it too. So, we are practicing what we preach.

Q. ***I've heard problems with Zoom and security. How is this addressed, and do you recommend we still use Zoom?***

A. As you know, Zoom has been flooded with new users because of the shutdown. Everyone is going online and going virtual. So, Zoom has since instituted passwords for your protection. You can do a one-time password per session. So, unless a hacker is really hell bent on getting into your session, which I don't know why they would be, a password is plenty enough to defer them. I literally use Zoom every day for various things I do and every day, it seems, Zoom is adding new features and making it more secure. Just today I saw a new feature in Zoom which is called a security connection. What I am saying, is, I wouldn't worry about security issues with Zoom. The stakes for them are incredibly high and so they need to ensure it is secure.

In my opinion, Zoom is a great platform for lots of reasons. You can share your screen by video. You can share a virtual whiteboard. You can share documents and you can send URLs. You can do a lot and it's not expensive at all.

Q. *What if a client is uncomfortable being on video?*

A. Good question. Some of the attorneys I've spoken to, they've asked me this. One great thing that you can do is if a client is uncomfortable, you can say to them, "You know what, I'll be on video. You can turn your camera off if you like. I don't need to see you. I'm the one presenting to you anyway and we can still go through your case evaluation."

That's a good fix. Again, it needs to be you, the attorney, not necessarily the potential client on the camera. Letting potentials know this will make people a lot more comfortable.

Q. Do you have recommendations for cameras and lighting and whiteboards?

A. I use an HD camera I purchased on Amazon. It was only around $80 or so. You can always use the standard camera that comes in a laptop too if you have to, but I highly recommend getting an HD cam. Don't wait if you don't have one. Use what you have and go ahead and order one. Another tip has to do with lighting. You want to have overhead lighting. If you can, I would get a bright lamp and put it up so that it shines on your face behind your computer. I have that and it makes your face look a lot better than just light from above. They are about $100 to $200 but that is icing on the cake. The point is to do presentations on video. Period. Lights or no lights.

Also, you should get a big whiteboard and use it landscape versus portrait for setup. As I recommend in the VCS, often you will need to diagram the case out. Those timelines tend to be easier to write out when your board is positioned landscape rather than vertical. When it comes to the markers you should use, make sure they are not faint. Use thick, black, green, red or any other easily seeable colors. If you have horrible handwriting, it's okay to go a bit slow. Just write clearly for people and again, dress professionally. Wear a shirt and a tie or at least a nice collared shirt. It shows people that you are serious.

Q. I've been practicing for 19 years. Older clients are my typical client's age range. Will they be able to use Zoom?

Zoom is pretty easy. There is something called Zoom phone that you can get if you want. It's a VOIP phone or a voice over internet phone and you can seamlessly transfer to Zoom even if they are just calling in by phone. Most people are calling in by smartphone anyway so you can send them a link via text or by email and they can just click the link and call in. So, to answer the question, there are ways to get anyone on Zoom, even if they don't know how to use technology well.

Q. Are there guarantees with the Virtual Close System?

A. No. I don't make guarantees because people may not use it. They may buy it and then not use the system fully and not give it an honest try. As attorneys you know that it's unethical to offer guarantees, so I don't offer them either. But I can tell you if you faithfully use the system, I just cannot imagine that you won't make your investment and more back. This system is fantastic. I know if you just start using it, you are going to be delighted.

Like I said, you can also apply the methods you learn in the VCS to existing clients as well. Even though it is ideally for potential clients, there is a lot you can do with it outside of that scope.

Again, there is no formal guarantee this will work for you. However, if you use it, I think you will really succeed, and you will be thanking me for it.

Q. I have heard you talk about payment plans and a bonus module. Can you go into that?

A. There is a company that I have worked with for quite a while called iQualify Lending. Jason Brown and Josh Eustace are the co-owners.

The bonus module that you will read about later is an interview with them and I go into a lot more detail on offering payment plans through their business. They have a lot of attorneys that they work with and their best attorneys are offering payment plans to everybody right now.

According to the data Jason and Josh gathered from Cleo, attorneys who are offering a payment plan right now are closing up to 47% more often. I don't get paid from their company if you sign up with them. I believe in what they are offering so much that I've included information on what they do in this bonus module.

In a nutshell, iQualify Lending allows you to offer payment plans to your potential clients. The client is funded through their company and you get your full retainer minus, a small fee within 72 hours. That way you can just focus on the legal work. They take responsibility for the payment plan with the client and it separates you from having to worry about it. For example, if the client can't pay for some reason, you don't have to withdraw from the case. You keep doing your job. It is not your role to follow up and collect the funds.

If you are using the *Virtual Close System,* combined with the follow up module and are also able to offer financing to potential clients, you will be leaps ahead of your competitors.

Q. *My staff person has been with me for 24 years. She is going to be resistant to using scripts*.

A. I've heard that one before. The answer to that is, you need to have people who are willing to use and follow the scripts. They don't have to follow it word for word. Anyone who is utilizing the scripts can easily put it into his or her own words. If they are still not willing to do it, you have to reconsider whether you can keep someone on who isn't willing to change and grow. They are now a liability to you at a time when you can't afford that. Is this person really invested in your success even if they've been with you for 20 plus years? I say no. I've had to let people go who have been with me a long time because of this exact type of thing. And you know what happened? I found someone who was 10 times better. Like you may be thinking now, I was wondering why hasn't done it sooner. This has happened to me dozens and dozens of times. If I have someone that's resistant and doesn't want to go with the program, I get rid of them. If I let them go, I'm happy I did and usually kick myself for not having done it sooner. It's a hard choice sometimes but you must do what is best for your business.

I encourage you to look at this in your own office. If you have people resistant, that means they are not going to help you when the chips are really down. Those are going to be the first people that run and close the escape hatch on you and let you drown unfortunately. I know this sounds harsh but it's true.

Q. ***I work B2B with small businesses. Will this work for me?***

A. I can't see a practice area that wouldn't benefit from the VCS. We do have a couple of clients that do B2B. We have two that have been using the *Virtual Close System* and the feedback so far has been good.

Again, even if you use the methods in the system for existing clients and not just potentials, having them hear you, see you and get to know you more personally never hurts.

NOTES

Made in the USA
Las Vegas, NV
03 November 2026

57424220R00171